ADVANCE PRAISE FOR *THE CHINA CHOICE*

The future of the US–China relationship is the single most significant and dangerous international issue of our time. Hugh White's book is a brilliant and incisive analysis of that relationship and contains vitally important recommendations for how its dangers may be avoided and peace secured. It is indispensable reading for both policy-makers and students of current affairs.

ANATOL LIEVEN, King's College London, author of *America Right or Wrong: An Anatomy of American Nationalism*

Hugh White's book offers the finest synthesis to date of all the major questions facing East Asia. It is a provocative work imbued with intellectual integrity. It is about the biggest question in international affairs – the future relationship between the United States and China. And the author's conclusions will satisfy no one, which is as it should be.

ROBERT D. KAPLAN, chief geopolitical analyst for Stratfor and author of *Monsoon* and *The Revenge of Geography*

This thoughtful, thought-provoking and highly readable book by a leading expert on Asian affairs cogently lays out the rationale for a power-sharing accommodation between the United States and China in East Asia, despite the inherent difficulty of the task and the wrenching changes in existing relationships that would be required. In doing so, the author provides a coherent and closely reasoned framework for informed thinking about the policy challenge for the United States of China's re-emergence as a great Asian power.

J. Stapleton Roy, director of the Kissinger Institute on China and the United States and former US ambassador to China

White marches us through the hard strategic implications of sustained economic growth in China. Clear and compelling.

Ross Garnaut, former Australian ambassador to China

Because I see many so many aspects of Chinese – and US – policy in a different light from the one Hugh White sheds on them in his book, I am the more sincere in urging attention to his analysis. Americans in particular will find it valuable to consider this trenchant assessment from a sympathetic but clinically detached perspective. Agree or disagree in the end, readers will be better off for understanding White's case.

James Fallows, national correspondent for *The Atlantic* and author of *Postcards from Tomorrow Square: Reports from China* and *China Airborne*

Every student of Asian geopolitics will benefit from reflecting on the arguments in *The China Choice*.

WALTER RUSSELL MEAD, editor-at-large of *The American Interest*

Hugh White makes a compelling case for the United States and its allies accepting that treating China as a power-sharing equal is the only rational response to its breathtaking rise. His detailed prescriptions leave much to contest, but the core argument – that any continued assertion of American primacy in Asia is bound to end in tears – is almost unanswerable. *The China Choice* makes a lucid and hugely stimulating contribution to a debate we can no longer avoid.

GARETH EVANS, president emeritus of the International Crisis Group

THE CHINA CHOICE

THE CHINA CHOICE

WHY WE SHOULD SHARE POWER

HUGH WHITE

OXFORD

UNIVERSITY PRESS

OXFORD
UNIVERSITY PRESS

Great Clarendon Street, Oxford, OX2 6DP,
United Kingdom

Oxford University Press is a department of the University of Oxford.
It furthers the University's objective of excellence in research, scholarship,
and education by publishing worldwide. Oxford is a registered trade mark of
Oxford University Press in the UK and in certain other countries

© Hugh White 2012

The China Choice was originally published in Australia by Black Inc.
This reprint is published by arrangement with Black Inc.

The moral rights of the author have been asserted

This edition published in 2013
Impression: 1

British Library Cataloguing in Publication Data
Data available

ISBN 978-0-19-968471-7

Printed in Great Britain by
Clays Ltd, St Ives plc

CONTENTS

For Jane

CHAPTER ONE
A HARD CHOICE

America and China are now the world's two richest and strongest countries. Their economies are deeply intertwined, and day-to-day business between them is generally managed well. But as China's power grows, there is an increasing undercurrent of rivalry that raises big questions about their long-term relationship, and what it means for the future. Will they find a way to live in peace with each other, or will they become strategic competitors – even enemies? Will Asia enjoy many more decades of peace and stability, or will it be devastated by conflict?

The answers are far from clear. Peace and stability are certainly possible, but the risk of rivalry and conflict is also quite real. Which it will be depends more than anything else on choices that will be made over the next few years in Washington and Beijing. Each country will have to decide how far it is willing to adjust its ambitions and aspirations to accommodate the other. Either one of them can push the relationship towards rivalry by asserting its ambitions too ruthlessly. Only together can they make the mutual concessions needed to pull back towards cooperation. Both, therefore, share responsibility for avoiding disaster.

This book is about America's part in that shared responsibility. The choices for America are quite urgent: Washington and Beijing are already sliding towards rivalry by default, seeing each other more and more as strategic competitors. The relationship between the world's two richest and strongest states will always be competitive; the question is whether that competition still allows them to trade and invest with each other, cooperate to solve shared problems, and contribute to maintain a stable international order.

Competition becomes dangerous when concerns about status and security become so intense that they preclude cooperation in other areas, and the quest for political, strategic or military advantage becomes the overriding priority. This is the path down which America and China are already taking the first steps. While for the most part their overt language remains cautious, they are building their forces and adapting their military plans specifically with the other in mind; seeking support from other Asian countries; and seeing regional questions, like the South China Sea disputes, more and more through the lens of rivalry. The further this goes on, the harder it will be to change course and choose cooperation.

America's choices about China are among the most important and difficult it has ever faced. They are important because serious rivalry with China would be very costly and dangerous, and conflict could be catastrophic. They are difficult because they touch on deep questions about America's role in the world, and therefore about America itself. China raises these questions because, in one fundamental way, it is different from any country America has ever dealt with: it is richer and more powerful. Within a few years China is set to have a larger economy than America, becoming the first country to do so since America overtook Britain in the 1880s. By mid-century, on some estimates, China's GDP could be double America's.[1]

China's wealth changes America's relationship with it because the old saying is right: ultimately, wealth is power. America itself has shown this to be true, with its global power built on its economic preponderance. Now China's swift economic rise is driving a rapid shift in relative strategic and political power. China still lags well behind America on many measures, but in almost every case the long-term trends are going its way. China does not even need to overtake America to pose a very serious challenge: its economy is already larger relative to America's than the Soviet Union's ever was. That makes China, in the long run, more formidable than the Soviets were at the height of the Cold War. And in Asia, where Chinese and American power meet, China enjoys many asymmetric advantages.

This growing strength confronts America with unprecedented choices. For forty years, both the US–China relationship and the Asian strategic order have been built on Chinese acceptance of America's superior power. At first this simply reflected a recognition of reality. When Nixon met Mao in 1972, China's economy was less than one-twentieth the size of America's. Beijing calculated then that it had no choice, in its own interest, but to accept an unequal relationship. In doing so, China relinquished its status as a great power in Asia, but only ever as a temporary expedient. Now that it is stronger, the calculations have changed. China believes it has the power to veto decisions it does not accept, and it is willing to use that power.

These are ultimately matters of status and identity. The Chinese feel towards their country, with all its achievements and for all its faults, in a way not so very different from the way Americans feel towards theirs. They, too, believe their country is exceptional and destined to lead. They see China as a great power. For nearly two centuries, China has been deprived of that status by other powers. Now that it has grown wealthy and strong again, nothing is more important to China than to reclaim its place as a leader in Asia. The Chinese will continue to avoid unnecessary friction and minimise the risk of confrontation. But they will not relinquish their country's claim to status as a great power – even if that leads to conflict. The implications of this for America are simple and very significant. If America tries to preserve the status quo and avoid fundamental change in the relationship, it will be choosing to accept China as a strategic rival.

The need for a decision seems to have emerged very suddenly. China's economic growth has been obvious, but not where it has been leading. Only a few years ago, serious people were talking of America as a new Rome, whose unchallengeable power would make this century even more an American Century than the last. America has been the world's richest and most powerful nation for so long that it seems inevitable, and essential to its nature, that it will remain so. It is indeed quite wrong to see America as a country in decline, because in itself America remains a remarkably vibrant and innovative society and economy. But it is equally wrong to imply, as American political leaders often do, that its relative position in the world of power is not changing.[2] This overlooks the simple mathematical fact that when we talk about relative power, America's trajectory is only half the story, and not the half that matters right now. The shift in power is being driven by China's rise, not by America's decline. There is not much America can do about it.

Likewise, it has been easy to assume that China will continue to accept the existing US-led global and regional order. China has appeared too preoccupied with economic growth and social stability to bother about challenging US leadership, and has not shown the ideological fervour or territorial appetites that have driven ambitious rising powers in the past. For reasons of its own, China has been happy for America to underestimate its power and ambitions as these have grown. But over the past couple of years, China's challenge has become clear, and so has America's need to decide how to respond.

Essentially, America has three options. It can resist China's challenge and try to preserve the status quo in Asia. It can step back from its dominant role in Asia, leaving China to attempt to establish hegemony. Or it can remain in Asia on a new basis, allowing China a larger role but also maintaining a strong presence of its own. Most Americans assume that the first of these options is the only choice. Only a few take the second option seriously, although that could change. Most don't even consider the third.

This book will explore the alternatives and in particular the third option, in order to argue that it is the one that best serves American interests. Many people doubt that the third option really exists. They assume that there are really only two alternatives. The argument goes that unless America maintains its benevolent leadership of Asia, the region will inevitably fall under Chinese leadership, which is likely to be much less benevolent. If that were true, America would have to choose between defending its leadership in Asia or surrendering the region to Chinese domination. The argument for defending the status quo would then be very strong.

I will argue that over the next few decades neither America nor China will be strong enough to lead Asia in the way America has done since 1972. Each will be able to deny leadership to the other. The hope that America can maintain uncontested leadership in Asia is therefore as illusory as the fear that China will be able to dominate Asia in its place.

In truth, any attempt by either Beijing or Washington to dominate will lead to sustained and bitter strategic rivalry, imposing huge economic costs and a real risk of catastrophic war. Neither side could win, and both would stand to lose a great deal – but it could easily happen. Strategic competition quickly builds its own momentum, escalating to the point where war can seem inescapable. War between the United States and China is already a clear and significant danger, one that will grow if rivalry increases. This is the most important issue at stake in America's China choice. Asia's alternative futures are not American or Chinese supremacy. They are escalating rivalry, or some form of great-power accommodation that constrains that rivalry. America's real choice is not between dominating or withdrawing from Asia: it is between taking China on as a strategic rival, or working with it as a partner.

The third option carries many obvious risks, which would quickly rule it out of contention were it not for the greater risks that flow from the alternatives. Moreover, this option can only be realised if America and China are willing to compromise with each other. Neither side will find that easy. For China it will mean abandoning hopes to lead Asia and accepting a strong US presence there indefinitely. For America it will mean accepting that its unique leadership role is no longer feasible, and learning to work with China as a partner in a way that America has never done with another country before – and certainly not with one so different from it. But this is the kind of choice America must now consider.

Much has been written in America about the US–China relationship in recent years, but relatively little of it explores

America's choices in these terms. Most writers conclude, or assume, that America will and should retain primacy in some form, and focus instead on China's choices. Many of them believe that China will in one way or another continue to accept American primacy. Others think that China will go the other way and challenge the United States. Some have acknowledged more explicitly the implications of shifting relative power, but without exploring precisely what America should do about it. Thus, while there is no shortage of books that explore the possibility of a looming clash between the United States and China, much less has been written about what America can do to prevent it.[3]

Meanwhile, in policy and political circles the ruling assumption remains that America must and will do whatever it takes to preserve its primacy. As the primary power, America might consult other countries, but it does not negotiate with them as equals. It sees itself as the only great power in the system. America's pre-eminent role in the Western Hemisphere under the Monroe Doctrine is a classic example of primacy, and we might say that America's primacy in Asia in recent decades has amounted to a kind of extension of the Monroe Doctrine to the Western Pacific. In particular, it precludes America dealing with China on terms of equality.

The widespread assumption that America's objective in Asia is to preserve its unique leadership role has had important consequences. As the scale of China's challenge has become clearer over the past few years, American policy analysts and leaders have found themselves accepting that rivalry with China is inevitable. Indeed, this emerged as the major theme of President Obama's first-term foreign policy – the so-called 'pivot' to Asia, shifting emphasis away from the War on Terror and the Middle

East, to strengthen America's position in Asia so that it can resist China's challenge.

This was spelled out starkly by the president in a November 2011 speech to the Australian Parliament in Canberra. The speech was the keynote of a nine-day trip to Asia intended to reassert American power. It was the first time an American president had acknowledged so clearly the scale of China's challenge, and set out so clearly an American response. After describing a future for Asia framed by America's values and interests, and after speaking dismissively of China's achievements and prospects, the president's peroration began:

> This is the future we seek in the Asia Pacific – security, prosperity and dignity for all. That's what we stand for. That's who we are. That's the future we will pursue, in partnership with allies and friends, and with every element of American power. So let there be no doubt: In the Asia Pacific in the twenty-first century, the United States of America is all in.[4]

The policy set out here by Barack Obama – it might come to be called the Obama Doctrine – is plain: the United States will resist China's challenge to the existing order in Asia with all the elements of its power. This is a declaration that America has made its choice about China, and the choice is for rivalry.

If this does indeed turn out to be the choice America makes about China, then Obama's speech may be among the most important in American history. But soon after the speech was given, it started to seem that the administration was having second thoughts. Paul Kennedy had already sketched an argument for accommodation with China, and in March 2012 Henry Kissinger wrote an essay in *Foreign Affairs* with the telling title

'The Future of U.S.–Chinese Relations: Conflict Is a Choice, Not a Necessity.'[5] Whereas his book *On China*, published in 2011, had seemed optimistic that a new relationship would evolve more or less painlessly, and without the need for America to make hard choices, the *Foreign Affairs* essay warned darkly of the risks of growing rivalry – including the risk of war.[6] 'A major war between developed nuclear countries must bring casualties and upheavals impossible to relate to calculable objectives,' he warned, saying that to avoid this state of affairs, the two countries must be willing to compromise to create a new regional order.

Also in March 2012, Obama's secretary of state, Hillary Clinton, gave a little-noticed but very significant speech to mark the fortieth anniversary of Nixon and Kissinger's historic visit to Beijing. Her tone was very different from the president's a few months before. She called for Washington and Beijing to negotiate their future roles. She said that this would mean 'a very different kind of relationship than the one we had.' It would 'require adjustments in our thinking and our actions, on both sides of the Pacific':

> We are, together, building a model in which we strike a stable and mutually acceptable balance between cooperation and competition. This is uncharted territory. And we have to get it right, because so much depends on it.
>
> Interdependence means that one of us cannot succeed unless the other does as well. We need to write a future that looks entirely different from the past. This is, by definition, incredibly difficult. But we have done difficult things before.[7]

Here we see the beginnings of a serious discussion about America's choices concerning China. This book aims to contribute to the discussion. It will do so by examining why America faces such a difficult choice and what the alternatives look like, and by fleshing out in some detail the option of negotiating a new deal with China.

Many questions need answers. What would such a deal look like? What would America have to give up? What would be demanded of China? What should America refuse to compromise on? How would it work in practice? The closer we look at these questions, the clearer it becomes that if China cooperates, America can continue to play a central role in Asia and live in peace with China. But it becomes equally clear that this can only happen if America makes some hard choices, soon.

CHAPTER TWO
AMERICA IN ASIA

UNCONTESTED PRIMACY

For forty years, since Nixon went to China in 1972, America has been the leader in Asia, and its primacy has been uncontested. The result has been a golden age. America has exercised more influence than ever before, and under its calming authority Asia has enjoyed an era of peace and prosperity unprecedented in its long history.

The consequences have been profound. After more than a century of conflict and dislocation, Asia took off. Since 1972 it has seen remarkable political evolution, social development, economic growth and regional integration, which together have laid the foundations for the Asian Century. American primacy has been central to this in several ways. It suppressed conflict in East Asia: clashes around the Spratlys notwithstanding, no major power has used significant military force in Asia since China attacked Vietnam in 1979. It suppressed the competition of major powers for influence over smaller powers, so that instead of competing blocs, an open and inclusive region emerged. It gave firm but gentle support to political reform and the evolution of democratic systems. And finally, it allowed Asia to join the US-led economic order in time to catch the wave of globalisation that has done so much to drive growth and social development. None of this would have happened without American leadership. Asia's success today therefore ranks among the great achievements of the American Century.

Uncontested primacy in Asia has also been central to America's own success. Not only has Asia's economic growth supported America's economy, but US primacy in Asia helped tilt the balance in the Cold War, contributing to the Soviets' eventual collapse. Strangely, all this followed America's failure in Vietnam, so that America's greatest military failure led to one of its great strategic successes. Two factors account for this.

First, although America failed to hold South Vietnam, the long struggle there shielded the rest of Asia from China's power at a critical time. The new countries of Southeast Asia, especially, had the chance to find their feet, to reject Chinese and communist models, and to start (sometimes very slowly) to move towards more open political systems and market-oriented economies. Richard Nixon, at least, understood this at the time. He argued that the war in Vietnam was important because it gave the rest of Asia breathing space. 'Whatever one may think of the "domino" theory,' he wrote in 1967, 'it is beyond question that without the American commitment in Viet Nam Asia would be a far different place today.'[8] Many in Southeast Asia would now agree.

Second, America's failure in Vietnam spurred the opening to China, because a deal with China was the key to bringing the troops home. America's way out of Vietnam led through Beijing. That was because, ultimately, Vietnam seemed from Washington to matter primarily as a piece in its strategic contest with Beijing.

If that contest could be called off, Vietnam could be let go – as indeed it was. So the need to get out of Vietnam was, along with the hope of Chinese support against the Soviet Union, a key reason why Kissinger and Nixon decided to offer China a deal to call off the contest. Their timing was good. China's domestic turmoil, economic stagnation and international isolation made it willing to do a deal that left America the uncontested leader of Asia – despite the fall of Saigon.

THE ROAD TO PRIMACY

The strategic heartland of Asia lies in its northeast. Today China, Japan, Korea and Taiwan together constitute one of the greatest concentrations of wealth and power on the planet, but Northeast Asia has always been a focus of strategic attention, and America has been engaged there for a long time. It was the first place outside the Western Hemisphere where America exercised sustained military power and built lasting political influence.

Europe's colonial powers found Northeast Asia a hard nut to crack. For centuries after they had taken control of the seas of Southeast Asia, their influence in the north was limited by the powerful governments of Imperial China under the Ming and Qing dynasties, and Japan under the Tokugawa shogunate. These were relatively coherent, effective and powerful states that for a long time resisted Western incursions. Only when the Industrial Revolution gave the countries of the West unprecedented power could they take them on, so the first decisive moves into Northeast Asia by Western powers did not happen until the 1840s, when the British launched an assault on the Qing Empire in the first Opium War.

Not long after, Commodore Matthew Perry of the US Navy sailed his 'black ships' into Tokyo Bay, so America was there from the beginning of the era of Western power in Northeast Asia. But it did not seek a great power role of its own in the region until the late nineteenth century. By the 1880s, having overtaken Britain to become the world's largest economy, America was building a big navy and so for the first time it had the capacity to fight wars in distant theatres. That became necessary because of the erosion of the nineteenth century's European-led global order. Europe's strategic balance was shifting sharply, as Germany emerged united and powerful in the heart of Europe, and Russian industrialisation started at last to harness the economic potential of its immense population. Britain's naval mastery was challenged as other European powers built big fleets, and the old Concert of Europe that had kept the peace between the great powers came under strain as competition among them intensified. The old order became less and less capable of managing conflicting interests either within Europe or in the colonial empires beyond it.

As this happened, the United States saw that it could no longer rely on the Europeans and would have to do more to protect its own growing interests beyond the Americas. Northeast Asia was where this need first became pressing. Japan quickly found its feet in the new world that was thrust upon it by the West, but China disintegrated. The competition of the European great powers with one another and with the newly emerged Japan over the spoils in China threatened what America saw as important interests of its own. The fate of China thus became the first issue of world politics outside the Western Hemisphere in which America took the part of a great power.

America's interests and motives were complex. Most obviously, Washington wanted access to the Chinese market. With their own continent now fully settled, American businessmen were starting to look beyond the Western Hemisphere for opportunities. Like the Europeans, they saw China's immense population as a vital new prospect, which would be closed to them if the Europeans had their way. But America's motives were not purely commercial. Its ideas about China had been shaped by the Christian missionaries who had flocked there for decades. Back home they promoted an image of the Chinese as a people eagerly receptive to American ideas – not just religious ideas, but political and economic ones too. With that image grew the conviction that America had a unique mission to raise China up and bring it into the modern world. China was the place where America could play its part as a 'civilised' country to bring the benefits of modernity to 'backward' societies, and do it not as a colonial power like the Europeans, but in a uniquely American way. Thus inspired, Americans wanted to save China from European colonialism and preserve it as an independent country in which this vision could be realised. Woven in with this genuine idealism was a strand of the same jingoistic nationalism that seized much of Europe around this time. Americans were very conscious of their great and growing power and deeply convinced of their country's unique moral quality, and many were eager for America to exercise its power on the world stage.

The avowed purpose of America's first strategic engagement in Northeast Asia was to support its 'Open Door' policy towards China. America opposed China being carved up by the Europeans and Japanese into colonial spheres of exclusive political and economic influence. Instead it wanted China to be preserved intact, open to all comers for economic opportunities, and encouraged towards reform and modernisation along American lines. This policy had a lot to be said for it. It took more account of the interests of the Chinese themselves than did the plans of the Europeans and Japanese. And it embodied the wider American aspiration for a new global order for the twentieth century, based on political independence, liberal ideals and free trade – very much the kind of order that it went on to create.

But the practical demands of power politics, the ineluctable lure of territory and the romance of empire also led America into its own experiment in colonialism in the Philippines. To play a major role in Asia, America needed a naval base there, and while other powers built their bases on territory seized from China itself, America looked elsewhere. War with Spain in 1898 provided the opportunity to annexe the Philippines, which not only offered a perfect place to base the US Navy, but also kept the country out of other hands, especially Germany's. By the turn of the century America was a fully fledged great power in Asia, ready and willing to compete on equal terms with the Europeans and Japan for influence. Its new weight was demonstrated when Teddy Roosevelt presided over the negotiations to end the Russo–Japanese War in 1905.

By then, however, the strategic balance was already changing, because European power in Asia had passed its peak. The shift was starkly symbolised by Britain's decision in 1904 to strip its Pacific Fleet of major warships, which were sent home to reinforce the Grand Fleet against Germany's growing naval power. And then, in 1905, a new strategic order in Asia was established when Japan's navy destroyed a Russian fleet in the Battle of Tsushima. This was the first time a Western power had been defeated at sea by a non-Western power since Vasco da Gama first brought European sea power to Asia.

Even before 1914, then, the era of European maritime primacy in Asia was past. The devastation of the First World War ensured it would never be restored. America was the only Western country still able to wield enough military power in Northeast Asia to shape political and strategic affairs, while Japan had emerged as Asia's only great power and America's only competitor in the region. Thus began a rivalry that lasted for forty years.

Japan came to see itself as the natural leader of Asia. By 1914 it had already acquired territory in Taiwan and Korea, and was ambitious to move into China. America, meanwhile, was determined to promote the Open Door and prevent Japan from dominating Northeast Asia. It saw Japan's ambitions as inimical to American economic interests; inconsistent with its hopes for China's future as a sovereign, modern and broadly pro-American state; incompatible with its Wilsonian visions for the peaceable conduct of international relations; and dangerous to the US position in the Philippines. More broadly, America had come to see itself as the natural and proper power to rule the waves of the Western Pacific, and the principal custodian of regional order.

Hopes that these differences between the two great powers could be bridged reached their peak in 1922 with the Washington Naval Treaty, under which Japan agreed to limit its naval forces to three-fifths the size of America's. This was bitterly resented in Japan, where it was seen as perpetuating the country's subordination to Western power. It strengthened those urging Japan to challenge the regional order, and helped set the path to war in 1941.

When war came Japan had the advantage that it was fighting closer to home, while America had to project force across the Pacific. But America's overwhelming economic preponderance outweighed Japan's geographic advantage, because US industry produced air and naval forces on a scale that the Japanese simply could not match. In May and June 1942, US forces started to win control of the Western Pacific from Japan in the great carrier battles of the Coral Sea and Midway, and that control grew relentlessly thereafter.

The defeat of Japan in 1945 left the United States as the dominant maritime power in Asia. Its aims there as the war ended were to preserve that position; prevent Japan's re-emergence as a competitor; nurture the evolution of China into a united, stable and broadly pro-American regional power; and limit the influence of the Soviet Union. It succeeded in all of these aims except, at first, in China. With the defeat of Japan, China's long civil war entered its last phase. The victory of the communists gave China, for the first time in a century, a central government in Beijing with effective and uncontested control over the whole of the country and the chance to re-establish the authority of the Chinese state. As Mao said, a century after the Opium Wars China had indeed 'stood up' again, as America had long wanted. But this had happened under a communist government closely aligned with Moscow and deeply hostile to the United States. In the phrase of the time, America had 'lost China,' and seemed on the way to losing Asia with it. For twenty years after 1949, China worked to exclude America from Asia, and to promote a region of communist states under Chinese leadership. America rejected that vision, denied the legitimacy of the Chinese Communist Party (CCP) as the government of China, and hoped to see the communist regime demolished.

China was, even then, a serious adversary for America in Asia. It was still very poor and technologically backward, but the sheer size of its territory and population gave it some of the attributes of a great power. Militarily, China's strengths matched America's weaknesses. America's position in Asia, like the Europeans' before it, has always been based on sea power, but it was relatively weak on land, where China's scale made it formidable. America has never fought a major successful campaign on the Asian mainland, and narrowly avoided major defeat at China's hands in Korea. In the 1950s, China's communist ideology was also an asset to some extent, because it still attracted support among some people in Southeast Asia. So for all its backwardness, China under Mao posed a significant challenge to America in Asia. After 1964 this was backed by nuclear weapons. Despite the massive disparity of resources, as the 1960s drew to a close, it was not clear that the United States would prevail.

THE DEAL IN 1972

This was the impasse that Kissinger and Nixon worked with Mao Tse Tung and Chou En Lai to break. In 1972 they reached what was in essence a very simple deal. America would recognise the CCP as the legitimate government of China, and China would accept America's role as the leader of Asia. There was also, implicitly but crucially, a third party to the deal – Asia's other latent great power, Japan. Like any good deal, this 'post-Vietnam' settlement among Asia's major powers looks obvious, sensible and inevitable in retrospect. But at the time it required all three parties to sacrifice major commitments and take significant risks, including domestic political risks, in order to achieve what we can now see were overwhelmingly beneficial long-term outcomes. Both China and Japan had other options in 1972, and had either made a different choice Asia would be a very different place today. Bismarck apparently once said that a statesman is a politician who thinks about his grandchildren: on that definition, this was a real display of statesmanship on all sides.

It is worth exploring their choices a little more closely, because they tell us something about the deal that has done so much to shape Asia today, and also offer pointers for the three major powers' choices in the future. At the heart of the deal were assurances given by Washington to both Beijing and Tokyo. In return for acceptance of US primacy, America assured China about its security from Japan and the Soviets, and Japan about its security from the Soviets and China. One might call it a double-double assurance deal.

For China's leaders, the 1972 deal meant abandoning their visceral aversion to what they saw as America's oppressive imperialism in Asia. More fundamentally, it meant shelving, for a time, their ambition to reassert China's status as a great power and their work towards restoring its leadership in Asia. These were major sacrifices, which went against key aspects of China's view of itself and its place in the world.

But in return China gained a lot. The most obvious and direct gain was insurance against its two most serious strategic threats, the Soviet Union and Japan. After 1972, China could be sure that Washington would not align with Moscow against it, and Moscow could not be sure that Washington would not align with Beijing against it. This greatly strengthened China's position against the Soviets. At the same time, Japan's continued subordination to America provided China with welcome assurance against the risk of a resurgent Japan.

Even more important in the long run were the economic dividends. American recognition gave China what it needed: an opening to the non-communist world, which alone could provide the capital, technology and markets that China needed to break out of the economic cul-de-sac of Marxist economics and start to grow. It is as certain as such things can be that without the opening to America in 1972, China would not be where it is today.

Politically, the deal with Nixon may have helped the process of political reform, which saw Mao's personality-driven, ideologically riven, factionalised and dysfunctional Communist Party transformed into the much more practical, technocratic, cohesive and effective party that has presided over the economic achievements of the past three decades. Still, in 1972 all these benefits were distant and hypothetical, while the costs were immediate and obvious. It could not have been an easy choice to make, or sell.

Japan's choices in the early 1970s were also difficult. The closing stages of the Vietnam War were deeply unsettling for Tokyo. At Guam in 1969, Nixon had announced that America would cut support to its Asian allies, and there seemed a real possibility that it might pull back from Asia entirely. These anxieties about US reliability were amplified by Nixon's visit to China, which naturally raised questions in Tokyo about how far it could continue to rely on Washington's support in any crisis with Beijing.

By 1972 Japan had well and truly regained its economic clout, and with it the potential to resume its status as a great power that it had relinquished after 1945. Some in Japan wondered whether it should indeed do this, in light of doubts about America. Since 1945 it had been America's strategic client, identifying its interests in Asia with Washington's, and depending absolutely on US forces for everything except the direct defence of Japan's homeland, and for much of that as well. If America could not be relied upon, Japan might need to regain its independence as a great power.

It didn't happen, of course. Japan opted to remain America's client and to vigorously support US primacy. This, too, delivered big benefits to Japan. It prevented the domestic and international ructions that re-armament would certainly have caused. It avoided spending much more money on defence. Perhaps most importantly, it avoided the risk that as an independent power Japan would be drawn into rivalry with China. By avoiding that, Japan was able to pursue the remarkable economic opportunities in China and throughout Asia which have been so important to it ever since.

Finally, the deal in 1972 carried both serious costs and immense benefits for America. The costs were obvious enough. By going to Beijing, Nixon and Kissinger had to reverse twenty-five years of policy and recognise the Chinese communists as the legitimate government of China. It is hard now to recall just how big a break this was. It followed two decades of bitter denunciation and two costly wars – in Korea and Vietnam – fought primarily to oppose Chinese influence. Probably only a president with Nixon's impeccably anti-communist credentials could have got away with it. Moreover, the Americans had to step away from the strategic commitment to Taiwan that had been a centrepiece of US policy in Asia since 1949. A compromise was only reached with Beijing over Taiwan at the price of deep ambiguities which have been a key point of friction in the relationship ever since, and may yet prove to be its downfall.

But for all these costs, the benefits to America of the 1972 deal have been immense – perhaps transformational. Nixon's deal with China and Japan did not just lead America out of Vietnam. It also aligned China with America against the Soviet Union and left US primacy in Asia uncontested. It left Asia set to follow a Western-oriented economic and political path, which made it, under America's leadership, the world's most vibrant region. After 1975, the Soviets never achieved – or even attempted – any substantial strategic gain in Asia east of Afghanistan. Indeed, one could argue that the Chinese economic achievement helped to push the Soviet Union over the brink by demonstrating what a well-run Leninist party could achieve, and thus showing up the miserable performance of the Communist Party of the Soviet Union. So, in his own way, Deng Xiao Ping probably did more to destroy Soviet communism than Ronald Reagan did. If so, Richard Nixon deserves some of the credit too.

AFTER THE COLD WAR

Beijing's response to the Tiananmen Square protests of 1989 posed the first serious test of the post-1972 relationship. It was a harsh reminder that China, for all its increased openness, remained a country with a sternly repressive communist government. The fall of the Berlin Wall later in the same year made the contrast between China and the rest of the world seem all the more striking, and to many it seemed unclear that China's system would survive, or that relations with the West could continue to develop. The economic relationship did not provide much ballast. A decade after China's economic transformation was launched in 1979, China was still a relatively small economy and few saw the scale of its long-term prospects. It remained a hard place to do business, and although it was beginning to be an attractive market for American companies, it did not appear central to America's economic future. Nonetheless, the administration of George H.W. Bush worked hard to minimise disruption to the relationship and preserve the central understandings on which it had been built. This seems to have been more a last application of old Cold War strategic logic than a first indication of new calculations.

In fact, as the Cold War ended, America's future in Asia seemed doubtful. To many people, it was far from clear that America would, or should, continue to carry the burden of leadership in Asia, now that neither China nor the Soviet Union needed to be contained. When Bill Clinton won the presidency in 1992, declaring, 'It's the economy, stupid,' these doubts seemed justified. Yet by the mid-1990s America had clearly decided to stay in Asia. One reason was that America emerged from the Cold War in better shape than most had expected. The economy boomed, and Americans grew confident that they had the power to lead, not just in Asia but around the world. With the Soviets gone, primacy in Asia was not very expensive, so long as it remained uncontested. And Asia itself was booming. In the 1980s its economic importance increased significantly. Japan's post-war economic miracle reached its zenith; Korea, Taiwan and many Southeast Asian countries grew strongly; and China launched the long boom that has built what will soon be the world's largest economy. America readily accepted that this was not a part of the world that it could afford to leave. And perhaps most importantly, over the 1990s Americans came to believe that the end of the Cold War offered a unique opportunity to consolidate their country's place at the head of the global order. It was obvious that leadership in Asia was essential to this vision.

Over the 1990s, as China continued to grow, the outlines of the present US–China relationship began to emerge. At one level – the level of day-to-day business – the relationship slowly developed a number of effective ways to handle the wide range of issues on which China became increasingly important to America as its economy and influence expanded. At a deeper level the relationship was increasingly framed by growing US recognition of the implications of China's growth for America's position in Asia.

By the mid-1990s there began to emerge what has turned out to be a very broad and enduring consensus about how America should respond to these deeper implications of China's rise. It gave rise to a policy known as 'hedging,' intended to prevent China upsetting the Asian order. The essence was very simple. Beijing was offered an implicit deal: as long as China accepted the existing Asian order and worked within it as what Robert Zoellick later called a 'responsible stakeholder,' America would help China to integrate into the global economy. But if Beijing challenged the US-led order by trying to expand its influence at America's expense – for example, by undermining US alliances in Asia or building forces that threatened the US military position – America would shift from engagement to containment, locking China out of the global economy and confronting it with the full weight of US power. This was a potent threat because for its own economy to grow, China needed access to the global economy for capital, technology, expertise and markets. In the 1990s America's pre-eminence in the global economic order seemed to give it the power to control China's access to these things. If China stepped out of line, America could simply close the gate and choke its growth. China therefore had a simple choice: accept American primacy and grow, or challenge it and stagnate.

The appeal of hedging was that, if it worked, any Chinese challenge would be self-defeating. Once it was locked out of the global economy, China's power would dwindle and its challenge would evaporate. The weakness of hedging was the largely untested assumption that China would never grow so vital to the world economy that it simply could not be locked out. The risk was that China might seem to go along with American leadership until that point was reached, and only then, when it was too late for America to swap from engagement to containment, would it let its ambition show.

This, of course, is exactly what happened. The bigger China grew, and the more closely it became integrated with the economies of other countries, including with the United States itself, the more unrealistic the policy became. By the start of the twenty-first century, China was probably already too big and too important to America and the global economy for Washington to be able to close the gate and lock China out.

This reality dawned only slowly in Washington. It took the Global Financial Crisis of 2008–09 to convince many people of how big and important China's economy had become, and how unrealistic the threat of economic isolation was.

But as the credibility of economic isolation has faded, the idea of strategic containment has taken over. Here the key assumption is that China needs peace and stability to grow: Beijing cannot afford the turmoil that would ensue if China tried to compete with America strategically. But the same problem applies: today America needs China as much as China needs America, and the costs of turmoil and conflict would fall just as hard on Washington as on Beijing.

So America's policy of hedging towards China has failed. America did not see how the challenge to its primacy was developing, and it was not willing or able to take the actions required to stop it. Now it is too late. America can no longer credibly threaten China with economic isolation or strategic containment to dissuade it from challenging US primacy.

How did this happen? One answer is 11 September 2001. For the decade afterwards, as China grew, America's attention was elsewhere. But perhaps a deeper reason is the view of the world, and of America's place in it, that had evolved since the Cold War. Most people believed that America's place at the head of the global order had become unchallengeable. Under US leadership, the core of the global system had entered a long and perhaps permanent era of stability, and the only threats to global order and US leadership would come from weaker players at the periphery of the system – such as failing states, rogue states and terrorists.

Future historians will wonder how so many could have been so blind as not to see the many ways in which this was wrong. The answer may be that most of us have found it impossible to comprehend the scale, speed and significance of China's rise.

CHAPTER THREE
CHINA: POWER AND AMBITION

THE POWER OF NUMBERS

Many people believe that America's economy will always be the biggest in the world. They say that America's economic pre-eminence has seemed under challenge before, most recently in the 1980s from Japan. 'Look at Japan now,' they say, confident that the challenge from China will go the same way, just as all the others have. But China is different. China's challenge to America's economic pre-eminence could succeed where others have failed because China has something the earlier challengers lacked: a workforce larger than America's. This makes all the difference.

The arithmetic is simple. Japan's workforce is only about one-third the size of America's. The average Japanese worker would therefore need to produce three times as much as the average American worker for Japan to overtake America's output. That was never going to happen, because America's combination of skills, technological innovation and entrepreneurship means its workforce is always going to remain among the most productive in the world. So the old prediction that Japan would overtake America was always going to be wrong.

China's workforce, on the other hand, is four times the size of America's. That means China's output will overtake America's when the average Chinese worker produces just one-quarter as much as the average American worker. Thirty years ago the gap in productivity between the average Chinese worker and his American counterpart was so immense as to seem unbridgeable, vastly outweighing China's greater numbers to give America a far greater GDP. China's remarkable achievement since 1980 has been to close the gap. It is now within reach of the critical point at which the greater value produced by each American worker will no longer be big enough to outweigh China's huge workforce. At that point China will have the largest economy in the world.

We are all surprised by how quickly this has happened, but the trends have been clear for a long time. We ignored them because we tend to forget that economic primacy is ultimately just a question of arithmetic, not an index of national character. GDP is determined by a simple sum: the amount produced by each worker, multiplied by the number of workers. America has had the world's biggest economy since the 1880s because it has had by far the biggest workforce in the developed world. Its workforce is now larger than all but those of two countries in the developing world, China and India. America has therefore been able to multiply the developed world's high per capita productivity across by far the largest number of workers.

Of course America's remarkable strengths as a country, as well as its natural endowment of a huge rich territory, have made this possible. Its openness, opportunity and freedom have attracted the millions of immigrants who swelled its numbers. Its innovation, entrepreneurship and creativity have kept its workforce among the most productive on earth, making it virtually impossible – as Japan found – for any smaller country to outpace it far enough on productivity to offset the size of America's workforce. This means that America's economy can only be overtaken by China or India, with their larger workforces, and only if they can approach American levels of productivity. And that is exactly what is happening.

If we take the long view, the rise of India and China today is less a revolution than a restoration – a return to normal after a two-century interlude. These were the two biggest economies in the world before 1800 simply because of demography. In that pre-industrial era, productivity was pretty much the same everywhere, so the relative size of economies was determined by the relative size of populations. Then the Industrial Revolution broke this simple linkage between population and GDP by creating what economic historians call the 'Great Divergence' in productivity. Per capita output shot up in a few advanced countries, and hardly moved in the rest. China's economy was overtaken for the first time in the early nineteenth century, when British workers became so much more productive than their Chinese counterparts that 20 million Britons produced more than 380 million Chinese.

Now the rest of the world is catching up. Future historians will be less surprised that this is happening in the early twenty-first century than that it did not happen much earlier. The 'Great Convergence' is driving per capita output in many parts of the previously 'undeveloped' world through the same kind of industrial revolution that Western Europe and North America experienced 200 years ago. The huge gap in productivity is closing, so that economic scale increasingly depends on workforce numbers. The two largest countries are therefore naturally moving towards becoming the two biggest economies, and China is in the lead. China started sooner and has moved faster, and for the time being its workforce is bigger than India's, so for the next few decades China is the country that will challenge America at the top of the global economy. In fact, it could grow much bigger than America before India overtakes it.

Nonetheless, though the arithmetic may be simple, the reality that China's economy could overtake America's is hard to grasp. America has been the world's richest country for far longer than anyone can remember, and the entire world has been shaped by the power that America has exercised as a result. We can hardly imagine the world any other way. Equally, we have never seen a country of over a billion people break out of poverty, join the modern economy and move towards OECD levels of per capita income. We have no experience of what such a country will be like, what kind of power it will have, and how it will behave. No wonder our initial reaction has been disbelief, and indeed denial.

In these circumstances, analysis often gives way to wishful thinking. For about the past fifteen years, ever since China's rise started to ring the first faint alarm bells, we in the West have erected an elegant three-tier hierarchy of mutually reinforcing beliefs about China to justify the conviction that its challenge does not need to be taken too seriously.

First, China's economy will not keep growing.

Second, even if China's economy does keep growing, it will not be able to convert economic size into political and strategic weight to match America's.

Third, even if China does build political and strategic weight, it will not choose to use it to challenge American leadership of the international system globally, or in Asia.

To understand the seriousness of the choices America faces, we need to explore why each of these propositions is likely to be wrong.

WILL CHINA KEEP GETTING RICHER?

The first question, of course, is whether China will keep growing. That is by no means inevitable. Its economic miracle could
slow, stop or go into reverse for all kinds of reasons. First, there
are the inherent weaknesses in its economy. In the near future
China faces formidable economic challenges, including inflation,
unsustainable levels of capital investment and a lot of potentially
bad debt. These will have to be managed at the same time as
China undergoes a fundamental shift from growth driven by
investment and exports, to growth driven by domestic consumption. It is quite possible that China's growth will slow significantly
over the next few years as it works through these problems –
even though the Chinese system has shown a formidable capacity
to manage such issues well in the past. However, even if they turn
out to be quite severe, these short- and medium-term problems
will not change the long-term shift in relative power between
the United States and China.

Consider the long-run trends. The rapid rise in Chinese productivity, which has driven its economic achievement over the
past few decades, has happened because hundreds of millions of
Chinese workers have moved out of semi-subsistence jobs in
agriculture, where their work was worth only a dollar or two a day,
into jobs in factories where their work is worth twenty or thirty
dollars a day. China's record in this is not remarkable. It is simply
following the usual trends of a country in the early stages of industrial revolution, where that first step from farm to factory yields
the biggest productivity dividend. China has the capacity to
maintain very strong growth because it still has several hundred
million rural poor in two-dollar-a-day semi-subsistence jobs, who
are available to take that first step into a factory and deliver that
big dividend. Their still-unrealised economic potential – if it can

be unlocked – provides the basis for China's economy to maintain strong long-term growth for some time to come.

But this human resource is not unlimited, and looking even further ahead there is no doubt that China's economy will grow more slowly as it matures. The World Bank, for example, estimates that it will slow from an average growth of 9% or more since 1980 to 5% in the mid-2020s.[9] By then the bulk of China's workforce will be in more productive jobs, and future growth will depend either on finding more workers or on achieving further increases in productivity beyond that first, easy step.

Demographically, the news for China is bad: its workforce is predicted to start shrinking within a few years, although it will still have the world's largest workforce for decades to come. This means that as its economy matures, long-term growth will increasingly depend on productivity gains. The Chinese understand this very well: it explains their massive investment in education. China is laying the foundations for future economic growth by building the capacity to increase the skills of its workforce. So while China's growth will slow, the economic fundamentals give no reason to assume that it will stop, let alone go into reverse. It might, but don't bet on it.

Of course, economic fundamentals are not the only factors that determine future growth. China could stumble for other reasons. One obvious problem is the environment. Thirty years of blitzkrieg industrialisation has had a predictably devastating effect on many parts of the country. Beijing takes this very seriously, and is spending a lot of money to fix existing problems and prevent new ones. That all comes at a cost and will have a long-term effect on growth, but there is no reason to believe that it will affect China's economic trajectory enough to reverse the long-term shift in relative power China's way.

There are much bigger questions about the global implications of China's growth. It is not clear that the planet can support another 1.4 billion people living the way we in the West live, with our levels of consumption of energy, food and resources. China is already the world's largest consumer of natural resources of all kinds, and this will only grow along with its economy. As other big emerging countries, especially India, follow China's path, they too will add hundreds of millions of new consumers, making unprecedented demands on the world's resources.

The control of carbon emissions is one obvious and critical problem. Others include how supplies of energy, water, minerals and other resources will be found, secured, allocated and priced. Such questions are critical to China's future economic growth, of course, because it cannot grow without resources. But when we think about the implications of this for China's *relative* economic position, it is important to bear in mind that this is everyone else's problem as much as it is China's. No country can take its access to resources or its level of carbon emissions for granted. If such issues are managed by international agreement, we can expect the costs to be shared more or less equally. If it comes to a scramble, China will be as well placed as anyone to secure access to the resources it wants, either by paying high prices or, if markets break down, though political influence or even – though this is much less credible – through military force. Whatever happens, there is no reason to assume that limited resources will slow China down any more than it slows anyone else.

Finally, there is politics. The biggest question hanging over China's economic future is whether its political system can manage the stresses of growth. There has always seemed something odd and unsustainable about a communist party presiding over a booming market economy. It has been natural to expect that the inherent contradictions between communist politics and market economics would sooner or later strain the Chinese system to breaking point. Certainly, no country has grown as fast as China for so long, or become as rich as it is today, under a political system as authoritarian as China's. Elsewhere, economic growth has forced major political changes, bringing greater individual liberty, wider political representation and stronger rule of law. Why should China be any different?

This is an important issue, but we should not oversimplify it. There is not just one political model for economic success. Every country going through an industrial revolution since the late eighteenth century has changed politically, but they have all evolved in unique ways, producing very different political systems. Compare Georgian Britain, mid-nineteenth century America, Bismarck's Germany, Meiji Japan and Lee Kwan Yew's Singapore. The differences are at least as striking as the similarities. Each had a quite different model for the relationship between government and the private sector, widely varying mechanisms of popular representation, and strongly contrasting ideas of personal liberty. This suggests that the political preconditions for economic success may not be as tightly defined, or as close to contemporary ideas of Western democracy, as we sometimes assume.

China's own experience tends to confirm that. For thirty years, ever since China's growth spurt started, we in the West have been expecting a collision between its political and economic systems. For thirty years the CCP has avoided that collision and managed to maintain both its own political position and China's economic momentum. This past success is no guarantee against future failure, but it does make it unwise to assume that political disruption will stop China growing.

One reason China's political system has survived thirty years of fast growth is that it has changed a lot. The CCP is very different today from the institution that Deng Xiao Ping and his colleagues wrested from the Gang of Four in the mid-1970s. It has abandoned not only Marxist economics but the rest of communist ideology as well, retaining only the core Leninist idea of one-party rule. It has preserved its monopoly of political power not only by brutal repression, but also by avoiding many of the mistakes that usually make authoritarian political systems so fragile. For example, unlike most one-party systems, the CCP has become quite good at acknowledging and addressing problems. China makes mistakes like anyone else, but it is fair to say that in recent decades the CCP has delivered standards of policy-making and implementation at least as good as those of more liberal-democratic systems. Likewise, most authoritarian systems are bad at leadership transition. The CCP seems to have developed a workable leadership model which avoids personality cults and bitter factionalism, and allows succession to be managed fairly smoothly. The transfer of power to the fifth leadership generation in 2012 suggests that China's politics are becoming more interesting and a little less stage-managed, but the system does nonetheless seem to provide stable and effective leadership.

Nonetheless, China remains a classic Leninist one-party state. The CCP is ruthless in preserving its monopoly of political power, and no system as repressive as China's has ever survived long in a country as rich as China has now become. Does this mean that the Chinese system is headed for the rocks? Not necessarily. Rather than presaging its downfall, the fact that no Leninist state has ever grown as rich as China might cut the other way and explain why its political system could survive. Nothing builds legitimacy like prosperity. No previous Leninist political system enjoyed the legitimacy that only economic growth can bestow. Perhaps China's political leadership will be the first of its kind to retain power over a successful modern economy, because it has been the first of its kind to build a successful modern economy and deliver so much prosperity to its people.

The people of China have a lot to complain about. Dissatisfaction with the CCP is widespread and growing. But this does not of itself mean that the present political system is unsustainable. For all their complaints, it is possible that most Chinese will grudgingly accept that the CCP's monopoly of power, with all its faults, is better than any likely alternative. If the CCP can continue for another few decades to evolve and adapt, keep China's economy growing, and find other ways to keep its people acquiescent, then it might keep its Leninist grip on the levers of power. Stranger things have happened.

Well, perhaps. It is also possible that China's growing middle classes will not be content to leave the government of China to the CCP, and will claim a larger role for themselves in debating and deciding their country's future. China faces some big decisions in coming decades, not only about the direction of its economy, but also about social, environmental and – as we shall see – foreign policy questions. The CCP will find it hard to persuade an increasingly comfortable, self-confident and well-informed people that the Standing Committee of the Politburo always knows best how to make these big decisions. Pressure for major political change in China could very easily grow.

What would that mean for China's stability, and for its economy? That depends on how hard the Chinese people push for political reform, and how hard the CCP resists. Many people who expect China's political problems to forestall its rise to power assume that popular pressure for reform will become irresistible, and that the CCP will remain immovable. If that happens, the prognosis for China is dark indeed – an escalating series of political crises in which the confrontation between the CCP and reformists in Tiananmen Square in 1989 is repeated on a larger and larger scale until the political system breaks down completely and China's economic growth grinds to a halt. This is clearly possible, but it is not the only possibility. It is also possible that pressure from below for political reform will meet some reluctant and halting willingness in the CCP to concede gradual liberalisation. If so, China's political system could evolve slowly but relatively peacefully towards something more sustainable.

For that to happen, the Chinese people would need to be patient and keep their demands for liberalisation rather modest, and the CCP would need to be willing to relax its grip on power. This would not be easy, but nor is it impossible. The Chinese people have a great stake in political reform, but they also have a great stake in stability and economic growth. It is probable that the majority of Chinese people are not so desperate for liberalisation that they are willing to risk political turmoil and economic collapse. Likewise, the CCP has a great interest in holding on to power, but it also has a great interest in avoiding catastrophic disorder. It is quite possible that, if and when the CCP leaders realised there was no alternative, they would be willing to surrender enough of their political monopoly to prevent a revolution. Such an accommodation is unlikely to be achieved without major crises and jarring confrontations, but the result could be the emergence of a new political settlement in China, which maintains order, expands liberty and keeps the economy on track. To assume that this is not possible – that the only alternatives for China are harshly repressive Leninism or chaotic revolution – is to overlook the capacity both of the

Chinese people and of the CCP to negotiate the evolution of China's political system in their own best interests.

In particular, it underestimates the stake that the Chinese people themselves have in their country's success. China is not like many other authoritarian countries. Its government is repressive, but unlike many repressive governments it has delivered genuine benefits to its people. In China today many hundreds of millions of people lead much better lives than their parents could have ever imagined, with better housing, better education, better healthcare, better clothes, more freedom to travel and better economic prospects. Only in the West, where we take such things for granted, do such momentous improvements in material welfare seem politically unimportant. Likewise, in the West we take political stability and order for granted. In China today many hundreds of millions of people are safer, and arguably enjoy more personal freedom, than any generation of Chinese before them. This is not to minimise or excuse the repression that persists in China, but rather to suggest that in assessing its political future, we should see how the present looks to the great majority of the Chinese themselves. There is today in China a great deal of dissatisfaction and dissent, but little appetite for revolution. The Chinese have too much to lose.

The bottom line? China's political system is under pressure, and it probably will have to evolve. But there is no reason to assume that this cannot happen in a way that allows China's economy to keep growing. That means America cannot rely on political turmoil in China to forestall China's rise and reverse the shift in relative power. Nor does it seem likely that economic, demographic and environmental pressures will slow China's economy sufficiently to halt its challenge to America in

Asia. China most likely will overtake the United States to become the largest economy in the world in the next few years. That will be a big psychological moment – for America and for China. When precisely it happens depends on how one measures GDP and whose numbers one believes, as well as on how the two economies perform. But by any measure it is very close, and may already have passed.

In 2011 the IMF predicted that China's economy would overtake America's by 2016, while the *Economist* went for 2018.[10] For our purposes it does not matter much. The stroke of the statistician's pencil will make little difference in practical terms. How strongly China keeps growing in future is already increasingly immaterial to the strategic choices that America faces today. China's economy has already grown enough to shift fundamentally the balance of economic strength between Beijing and Washington. China is already rich enough to challenge American primacy in Asia.

Nor is there any reason to assume that these trends will not continue to favour China. There is a real chance that it will not just overtake the United States, but grow to the point where, within a few decades, it is significantly wealthier. If China achieves OECD average levels of per capita income, it would have an economy three times the size of America's.[11] The possibility that this could happen within a few decades can no longer be regarded as fanciful.

WILL CHINA KEEP GETTING STRONGER?

China may be getting richer, say the sceptics, but is it getting stronger? Does its growing wealth provide it with the strategic and political power needed to challenge America in Asia? Many people think not. They argue that America's power reflects much more than the size of its economy. It springs from America's nature as a country, the strength of its institutions, its mastery of every major frontier of technology and its unsurpassed military predominance. GDP alone will not help China match all these. In recent years, as America's supremacy in GDP has eroded, quite a lot of effort has gone into arguments that GDP is at best only a partial index of national power. Clearly this is true to some extent. But it is a big step from there to argue that China's growing output relative to America's does not significantly shift the balance between them.

At heart this is a question about the nature of power. National power has many manifestations and can be exercised in many ways. But history suggests it has only one fundamental source, and that is sheer economic scale. No country has ever exercised great power without great wealth, and – with post-war Japan as perhaps the sole exception – no very wealthy country has ever failed to manifest its economic weight in strategic power. This is not to suggest that power is determined solely by wealth. A richer country will not always be more powerful, because some countries can convert wealth into power more efficiently than others. Much depends, as we will see later, on a country's circumstances and objectives, as well as its political, strategic, military and industrial skill and ingenuity. And while America undoubtedly has many such advantages, some of the more important differences between them favour China instead.

Let's start, though, by looking at China's record in converting its economic weight into other forms of power. First, and most obviously, China's economic growth has directly increased its political and diplomatic influence. The openness of its economy means that for many countries, both in Asia and beyond, China has become their most important economic partner, and growing trade with China, or aid from China, is central to their future. This makes a lot of countries sensitive to China's interests. Australia is a good example. China is not only Australia's biggest trading partner today; it is also seen as the locomotive for future growth. That gives Australia an immense stake in China's economic success, and in good relations with Beijing. The close connections between business and government in China make it easy for China to apply commercial leverage for diplomatic ends. Nor is there much reassurance in the fact that interdependence cuts two ways, because one side of the blade is sharper than the other. China does not depend on each of its trading partners as much as they depend on China. In the short term China might need to buy Australian iron ore and coal almost as much as Australia needs to sell them, but in the longer term China can find new suppliers more easily than Australia can find new customers as big as China. So Canberra, like so many other capitals, knows that to protect its immense trading interests, China's key concerns must be respected.

It has been easy so far to underestimate how much diplomatic clout Beijing has acquired in this way, simply because it has chosen not to use it much. For a decade or more its diplomatic strategy, especially in Asia, has been to allay its neighbours' inevitable anxieties and persuade them that there is no political risk in their growing economic dependence on China. Only in the last two or three years has China started to flex its muscles a little, and even so it is usually cautious not to allow other countries to see just how strong it has become. This reflects a second way in which China's influence has increased in recent years: it has become much better at the arts of diplomacy.

Until well into the 1990s, China's diplomacy tended to be wooden, doctrinaire and either hectoring or defensive. Since then, Beijing has developed a much more open and persuasive way of doing international business. Its diplomats are more fluent and engaging. China has become more effective at international gatherings, seeing them less as threats and more as opportunities, and has at times been surprisingly accommodating, willing to sacrifice short-term goals to cultivate the image of a benign and unthreatening power. Of course, China is still perfectly capable of harsh and hectoring diplomacy, and there remain issues – Taiwan, for example – where serious intellectual engagement is rare. China's recent hard line on the South China Sea has set back its diplomatic charm offensive in Southeast Asia quite sharply. But it would be wrong to imagine that China has no capacity, when it wishes, to present a persuasive case and build support for its positions through effective diplomacy.

Many people argue that America nonetheless retains a clear advantage over China in the 'soft power' embodied in the sheer attractiveness of its society, culture, institutions and ideas. China might be growing rich, the argument goes, but it remains hard to admire. This is surely true. Few outside China want to emulate it in the way so many want to emulate America. But it would be wrong to be complacent about this. The more China grows, the more attractive it will become. Chinese products will become more appealing, its movies will become more entertaining and its universities more attractive. America's political and business institutions have perhaps a little less gloss than when Joseph Nye first popularised the idea of soft power as the secret of America's future strength. And the historical precedents are not encouraging. As their economic primacy waned, the British put great faith in what they called their 'prestige' – by which they meant what we today call soft power – to offset the loss of more tangible strategic assets. Alas, they found it was not much help once the substance of wealth and power was gone.

Moreover, it is hard to know what soft power really does for America. How far will it help tip the scales America's way against China if rivalry grows and smaller countries in Asia face stark choices about how far to support America? Vietnamese, Indonesians and Australians certainly admire and trust America more than they do China. But will that make them support America against China, beyond what they see as being directly in their own interests? America's soft power might make other countries more likely to see their interests more closely aligned with America's than with China's, but it will not make them see their interest as identical with America's, and it will not make them put America's interests ahead of what they see to be their own. American soft power means that China's neighbours would far prefer America as the leader of Asia, but they will not support America against China further than their own interests dictate. And it would be unwise to assume that America's soft power will outweigh China's hard economic and strategic power in their calculations – as we will explore in Chapter Five. The balance of American and Chinese influence over other Asian countries is not necessarily as favourable to America as many assume.

The same could be said of the balance of military power. It is easy to assume that, whatever happens in other fields, America will remain overwhelmingly superior to China in military power, which remains the ultimate arbiter. Certainly America's defence budget is much larger than China's, its armed forces are far superior in quality and capability, and China simply cannot match America's unique capacity to project armed force anywhere in the world. All this will remain true for a long time to come. Although China's defence budget has grown rapidly over the last few decades, and is now second only to America's, it is still a lot smaller. Likewise, China's air and naval forces have grown quickly, but they are still smaller and much less capable than America's. So whether we look at what they spend, what they have now or what they are likely to have in ten or even twenty years' time, America remains way ahead of China as a military power.

But when we look not at what they spend or what have they got, but at what they can do where it matters most, the balance appears different. As we will see in Chapter Four, the military contest between the United States and China is very asymmetrical, and the asymmetries all tend to work in China's favour. America's military advantage over China is therefore narrower and more fragile than one might expect, and China has already gone a long way to erode it, thus undermining the foundations of America's primacy in Asia. That does not make America powerless, of course – a long way from it – but it does raise the costs and risks of confrontation. These trends will only be amplified by fiscal pressures on the US defence budget, and continued strong growth in China's.

WILL CHINA CHOOSE TO CHALLENGE?

China's economic growth is translating into growing strategic and political power. What will China do with it? One common view is that it will do very little. Some argue that China is not ready for leadership – for 'prime-time.' It is reluctant to accept the obligations and responsibilities that go with great power, and will be happy to leave all that to America. This may be half true. China shows little interest in asserting any leadership role beyond the East Asian and Western Pacific regions. But we should not mistake China's reluctance to shoulder the burdens of leadership, as they are defined by Washington, for reluctance to exercise power in pursuit of its own agenda. From Beijing's perspective, Washington's definition of the responsibilities of leadership reflects America's interests, not necessarily China's. China will not shoulder the burden of protecting the US-led international order where that does not suit its interests, but it will happily use its power to serve its own interests where it can. The Chinese are quite ready for prime-time, but they will sing their own song.

A stronger argument suggests that China will continue to accept the status quo in Asia because any challenge would be contrary to its economic interests. In a globalised world, economic interdependence makes it impossible for China to risk the consequences of strategic rivalry. Above all else, China's rulers must keep its economy growing in order to keep its people happy and the CCP in power. That requires a stable international environment and good relations with the United States. Hence China will continue to accept American primacy as the best way to maintain a stable international environment and keep relations with America in good shape.

There is some force in this argument. Certainly we can expect that Beijing will continue to place a very high priority on economic growth, and that requires international stability. This will have a strong influence on the way China exercises its power and approaches the management of relations with America. But the argument is mistaken in assuming that the desire for economic growth will be the only factor influencing China's thinking about its place in the world. China's priorities are more complex than that. Economic growth is certainly one goal for Beijing, but not the only one. China's rulers want their country to be wealthy, but they also want it to be strong and respected.

They want it to be a leader among nations. This is not new. When China's first generation of modernisers dreamed of pushing back against the Western powers in the mid-nineteenth century, they summed up their aim in a simple slogan: to make China 'wealthy and strong' and restore it to its old place at the head of the Asian order. It would be surprising if their successors in Beijing today do not share these ambitions.

It would be even more surprising if China's people do not share them too. Clearly the Chinese are no less patriotic than the citizens of any other country. As China grows richer and stronger, they are presumably eager for their nation to have a larger role, to exercise more influence among nations and be given more respect. If so, they are no different from the people of any other rising power. The people of Britain, America, Germany, Japan and the Soviet Union were all, in their time, ambitious for their countries to translate economic growth into international leadership. Why should we expect the Chinese to be any different? In fact, their ambitions are likely to be amplified by their intense and carefully cultivated sense of history. As they think of China's future place among nations, they must be deeply conscious of their country's extraordinary past, of its humiliation at the hands of the West and Japan, of its remarkable current achievements, and of its glowing prospects. No wonder Chinese patriotism often shades into nationalism and even jingoism – just as patriotism in other countries often does.

This means that when China's leaders make decisions about their country's relations with Washington and its role in Asia, they will not focus solely on what's best for their economy. Their ambitions for their country, and the expectations of their people, mean they will also give weight to what serves to build China's power, influence and status. This makes them no different to the leaders of other strong countries, including the United States; and like them, China's leaders will sometimes make decisions that they believe enhance China's power and status at the expense of its economy.

The key question is how Beijing will balance these imperatives when they conflict. How far will China be willing to risk its economic trajectory for the sake of political status and strategic weight? This is hard to assess. On the one hand, Beijing will understand that continued economic growth is vital to the credibility of China's political system, and in itself essential to expanding China's power and influence. But China's version of domestic politics will also press Beijing the other way. An increasingly proud, confident and nationalistic public will be impatient for China to use its growing strength to assert itself more forcefully, shape the regional order in its interests and resist more robustly anything that seems an infringement of its rights. China's leaders will not be able to ignore these popular expectations any more than they can ignore demands for sustained economic growth. Nor should we assume that they would always want to: China's leaders are probably just as ambitious for China, and just as impatient, as their people are.

So China faces a classic policy dilemma. It needs stable international relations to foster economic growth, but it also needs the international order to change to accommodate China's ambitions for power and influence. This dilemma is faced in different forms by all strong states – those who have the power to reshape their regional order if they choose. Great powers are always tempted to reshape the international order to increase their influence. But they also want to minimise the risks that flow from the instability and conflict which will result if they grab for power too greedily. So they have to balance their ambitions for influence with their desire for order. Only very rarely does a leader like Hitler or Napoleon pursue power with no regard for order. But it is even rarer for leaders or peoples to forgo all aspirations for power for the sake of preserving order – in fact, post-war Japan may be the only example we have.

As China's leaders balance these conflicting imperatives, they will probably continue to place a high priority on preserving political and strategic stability in Asia. But there is almost no chance that they will forgo all ambitions to expand their power and influence, and instead accept the status quo of US primacy indefinitely. That would mean China relinquishing its claim to the status of a great power and accepting a subordinate status to the United States, as it becomes the world's richest country. That will not happen. Moreover, Beijing's choice between maintaining economic growth and asserting power may not be as stark as it appears. China need no longer fear that America and other countries will deliberately exclude it from economic interactions if China challenges the regional order. As discussed in Chapter Two, this implicit threat was once central to the policy of hedging China's rise, but now China is too important to the global economy for it to be credible. Nor does China assume that without US leadership Asia is sure to collapse into chaos. Beijing can easily imagine that Chinese leadership would be just as good a basis for Asian order, and much better for China.

Indeed, in Beijing they might believe that a change of regional leadership would be better for China economically. In their view Washington was only ever going to support China's growth as long as it did not obviously threaten America's place in Asia. That is why China has downplayed its growing power and ambition. This was the point of Deng's famous injunction for China to hide its strength as it grew. Now the strength has become so obvious that Beijing fears that America will in future look for ways to use its leadership of Asia to limit China's growth.

From Beijing it may appear that China has reached a cross-over point. For decades American primacy in Asia has been good for China's growth, but in future years the opposite might be true. China has accepted US primacy for as long as Beijing believes that it works for China, and no longer. So China's restraint in not earlier claiming more power and influence as its economy has grown should not be mistaken for lack of ambition. Instead it shows patience, and perhaps a measure of guile. Time is on China's side. The longer it has waited to challenge Asia's US-led order openly, the stronger its position has become, and the better placed it is to shape what follows to its own purposes.

INTERDEPENDENCE

The view that China's economic interests will preclude it challenging America in Asia is often buttressed by a broader argument about the consequences of economic interdependence. Kant predicted over 200 years ago that as trade among countries increased, the costs of conflict would grow too, while the motives for conflict would dwindle. Eventually trade would make rivalry and war disappear. Some people think he has been proved right since the end of the Cold War. For twenty years, relations between the world's major powers have been notably stable and peaceful, coinciding with unprecedented globalisation and economic growth. It has been tempting to see this as the sign of a new international reality: globalisation causes the peace, and globalisation is irreversible, so peace in future is assured, at least between major powers.

Certainly, the more countries trade and invest with one another, the greater the economic cost of conflict and the stronger the incentive to keep the peace. America and China today are more interdependent economically than any two comparably powerful states have ever been before, and this will certainly restrain ambition and rivalry on both sides. The question is whether the restraints will prove stronger than the pressures going the other way. If interdependence does trump strategic and political ambition, we should be seeing it happening between the United States and China now – but we have not seen much evidence of that yet. So far the two countries seem to be acting very much as strong states in the past have acted as relative power shifts from one to the other. Pessimists like John Mearsheimer and Niall Ferguson remind us that before war broke out in 1914, the great powers of Europe had grown more economically interdependent than they had ever been before, and than they would be again for almost a century.[12]

The lesson to draw is that interdependence increases the incentive for leaders to subordinate political ambitions and ignore nationalist sentiments, but it does not remove the need for them to take these bold and politicaly risky steps. The hard choices still have to be made. It is easy for leaders to see that economic interests require them to compromise their countries' aspirations for international status and power, but it is harder for them to acknowledge that to their people, and harder still to put their economic interests ahead of strategic and political ones when a choice has to be made. In fact, most often people see it as shameful to put economic concerns first when issues of power and status are engaged. What president would tell the American people that their country will compromise its position on an issue like Taiwan in order to protect America's economic interests? What Chinese leader could make the same argument to the Chinese people? When a choice has to be made, especially when it has to be made in the glare of an international crisis, it is very hard to put economics first.

In some ways the obvious importance of economic interdependence increases rather than limits the risk that rivalry will escalate, because of the way it can affect one country's view of the other's priorities. There seems to be a pattern here: each side believes that the imperatives of interdependence will press more heavily on the other. That inclines both governments to assume that the other will compromise to protect the economic relationship, so they do not have to do so. In Washington they expect China to back down from its challenge to America once Beijing understands the economic risks of rivalry. In Beijing they think America will blink. That makes both of them less inclined to compromise their own position – which makes escalation more likely.

Ultimately, faith in the power of interdependence boils down to faith in the power of money to trump other emotions and motivations. That is a risky proposition. We cannot assume that Chinese leaders will always choose rationally to maximise China's objective benefits. They are no less liable than the leaders of any other country to allow what may be, or may seem to us to be, irrational desires for status and influence to trump the rational calculations of national interest.

Economics is important, but money isn't everything. Countries, like people, want to be rich, but they also want to be safe and to feel good about themselves. For countries, as for individuals, aspirations for security and identity often compete with material interests, and often win. America's and China's divergent visions touch on very deep issues of national identity in both countries, which can easily seem to outweigh economic imperatives when the crunch comes. And there is always something a little strange about the assumption, implicit in the interdependence argument, that our economic desires will suppress the urge to strategic and political competition when our desire to avoid the horrors of war will not.

WHY RIVALRY?

The deeper question remains: why would China want to challenge America for leadership in Asia? What does China want? We tend to look for material or ideological motives for conflict between nations, because that makes it seem more rational. Such motives are hard to find between the United States and China, which can lead to misguided complacency about the risks to the relationship. The most bitter rivalries often have the most intangible origins.

The most obvious source of rivalry between great powers is competition for territory. Optimists take comfort from the fact that – the special case of Taiwan aside – America and China have no directly overlapping territorial claims; indeed, China seems to have no territorial ambitions beyond its current borders. Pessimists point to the many disputes China has with its neighbours over the demarcation of these borders, including disputes in the South China and East China seas. The optimists reply that China has successfully managed and settled a number of these disputes, and that it is hard to see China making grabs for its neighbours' territory beyond the currently disputed areas. On balance the optimists are probably right about this. We cannot be sure how China's appetite will develop in future, but it is hard to see how its territorial ambitions provide a motive for conflict with America, in the absence of deeper factors.

Likewise with ideology. Those who grew up during the Cold War tend to see different world views as the most potent source of rivalry between great powers. Some people find this reassuring, because they do not see an ideological split between America and China that is comparable to the split between America and the Soviet Union. Others find it worrying, because they do see major ideological differences. Who is right? Clearly, China does not pose the kind of ideological challenge to America and the West that the Soviet Union and its communist partners did in the early stages of the Cold War. China may still be ruled by a communist party, but that party retains no trace of the evangelical fervour and internationalist ambitions of the communist parties of old. The CCP today makes no claims for communism as the answer to the world's problems or the key to the future of humankind. Nor does it try to use the ideology of communism as an instrument of political influence beyond its borders, as its Maoist predecessors did. It would fail if it did. Communism disappeared as a serious challenge to Western political systems long before the end of the Cold War, and seems unlikely to revive.

Indeed, it is hard to imagine that China's government today would have a foreign policy that is in any sense driven by communist ideology rather than Chinese national interests. That is because the CCP has largely dropped communist ideology itself. All that remains of the old Marxist–Leninist construct is rigorous adherence to one-party rule, adapted to serve the needs of China's unique model of state-infused market capitalism. To the extent that Beijing shows any signs of wanting to promote this model abroad, it seems to be as a half-hearted counter to what it sees as American ideological evangelism, rather than any real conviction that China would be served by others adopting the Beijing Model. This reflects an important difference between

America and China. Both regard themselves as exceptional, but while America sees its exceptional strengths and virtues as a model for others to emulate, China see its strengths and virtues as proof of China's inimitable uniqueness. Americans still hope everyone can become like America, whereas Chinese do not believe that anyone can become like China.

If they are not focused on territory or ideology, some people see competition for energy and other resources as a mainspring – perhaps *the* mainspring – of rivalry between the United States and China. They argue that the growth of China, alongside that of India and other big emerging countries, will increase demand for resources too fast and too far for supply to keep up, and the resulting tussles will shift from the commercial to the strategic arena.

But this does not seem to be what's happening, and fear that it might overlooks the way today's globalised economy works. In an earlier stage of industrialisation, trade in goods and resources flowed between metropolitan powers and colonies along defined lines. Trade followed the flag, and vice versa. One of the great achievements of recent decades has been to replace this constrained version of globalisation with a much more open system in which the flag has very little to do with trade. Trade follows price, quality and availability. This has not only made the world much richer, it has also made the world's largest economies deeply interdependent, to a degree probably never seen before. In today's world, how would China benefit economically from depriving America of iron ore, and how could America profit commercially by depriving China of oil? So long as economic considerations are uppermost in everyone's mind, and globalisation is not sharply reversed, interdependence will ensure that everyone cares about everyone else's economy almost as much as about their own. In effect, there is only one big global economy on which we all rely.

Naturally, if big countries like China and India keep growing, demand for resources and energy may well grow faster than supply, and perhaps further than the globe can sustain. That will pose titanic problems of allocation, but as long as the world's economy remains globalised, the market will do that for us through price. This might not be easy or pleasant – oil at a thousand dollars a barrel – but it need not be violent, so long as a relatively free and open market can be preserved. That means that in a globalised world, competition for resources is unlikely to be the engine of escalating conflict. In fact, as we will see, it is much more likely to be the *result* of strategic rivalry rather than its cause.

Thucydides wrote that the great sources of war are money, fear and honour. As we have seen, economic imperatives provide no reason for rivalry between America and China: just the opposite, in fact. Ultimately, their contest seems to spring on both sides from a combination of fear and honour. Today we might say 'security' and 'status.' China fears that if America remains the leader in Asia, it will use its power and position to limit China's growth, constrain its influence and undermine its political system. America fears that if China becomes more powerful, it will push America out of Asia, threatening America's global position and perhaps eventually threatening America itself. China wants to be accepted as a leader in Asia, perhaps as *the* leader, and certainly as a great power equal in status to America, partly because it believes that otherwise it cannot be secure, and partly because it sees such a status as essential to its identity. That is the kind of country China believes itself to be. America wants to remain the leader in Asia and to avoid acknowledging China as an equal because it believes that leadership is the only international role that is consistent with America's unique nature as a country, and that dealing with any country as an equal is incompatible with its exceptional nature.

We might wonder at the power of these beliefs and motives, but we cannot dismiss them. Throughout history, they have caused the world's biggest wars. Thucydides' explanation of the rivalry of Athens and Sparta still captures, as well as any, the forces at work. After discussing the specific events that led up to the Peloponnesian War, Thucydides wrote, 'The real cause, however, I consider to be the one which was formally most kept out of sight. The growth of the power of Athens, and the alarm which this inspired in Sparta, made war inevitable.'[13]

WHAT DOES CHINA WANT?

If I have persuaded you that China's challenge should indeed be taken seriously, two critical questions will now arise: how much power and status does China want? And what does it have the power to get? The gloomiest possibility is that Beijing might want to establish a harsh regime of control across Asia backed by armed force, much as Stalin did over Eastern Europe after 1945.

China's communist political system makes it easy to assume that its strategic objectives will follow Stalin's example. No doubt there are some people in China who would like their country to wield this kind of power, and their numbers may grow. The stronger China becomes, the more tempted it will be to try to subjugate its neighbours. Guarding against this possibility must always be a prime concern for China's neighbours and others with an interest in Asia's future.

Nonetheless, while we should recognise this risk, we should not exaggerate it. Much as it may grow, China has little chance of becoming powerful enough to impose a Stalinist-style dominion over Asia. There are too many other strong states in the region that will get in the way. Most obviously and immediately, it will face America itself. Japan, for all its problems, will be for many decades a country with great strategic potential based in a huge economy with great technological depth. India, if it fulfils its promise, will start to rival China's power before the middle of the century. Finally, Russia, though no match for China in raw economic scale, and unlikely to be a key player in the wider Asian system, will still be a formidably armed neighbour which China must always treat very carefully.

Beijing would find it virtually impossible to dominate Asia against the committed resistance of even one or two of these powers, let alone all of them. It could also face the resistance of several substantial middle powers, especially South Korea, Vietnam and Indonesia, who might well support the great powers in resisting a Chinese bid for hegemony in Asia. Against such opposition, China would find that instead of securing assured primacy over Asia, it would be mired in an open-ended, costly and ultimately unwinnable struggle from which it would emerge much the poorer, or even be plunged into a catastrophic war. So far these things seem well understood in China, which no doubt explains, better than any commitment to abstract principles of international relations, why China shows no signs of following in Stalin's footsteps.

This does not mean, however, that China has no ambitions to lead Asia. It simply means it is not looking to Stalin for a leadership model. Across the Pacific it can see a much better model in the Western Hemisphere, where America has claimed unchallenged leadership since 1823. Under the Monroe Doctrine, America has protected its core interests, excluded rivals and minimised threats to its security, without the costs of maintaining a harsh hegemony. The softer style of US leadership in the Americas has given Washington all the benefits of regional leadership at a fraction of the price, without major invasions or protracted military occupations. Though Chinese leaders seldom speak explicitly of their aspirations for leadership, this must be an appealing model. With its own 'Monroe Doctrine' in Asia, China could enjoy unquestioned leadership and great security, very cheaply, rather as the Imperial Court did in the days of the tribute system. It could be seen as a natural evolution of China's imperial system, and in a sense continuous with the era of uncontested US primacy just passing, which has been in effect an extension of the Monroe Doctrine to the Western Pacific.

But can they do it? Could Beijing persuade the rest of Asia to accept China, not as a harsh overlord but as a firm but kindly elder brother? This is the great challenge facing Chinese statecraft. Lacking the power to dominate Asia by brute force, can it assert regional leadership by a deft combination of persuasion and pressure? This is where soft power really counts. America has enjoyed uncontested primacy because countries throughout Asia have trusted it not to misuse its power to infringe their key interests. China has been working for over a decade now to cultivate the same kind of trust for itself, but it has not been wholly successful. While China is generally quite well liked and respected in Asia, deep reservations remain, and the more forcefully the Chinese assert their ambition for leadership, the less other countries are willing to entrust them with it. There is always the fear that what might start as soft Monroe-style Chinese leadership would slide into Stalinist aggression.

These fears are strongest in the Asian country that China most needs to convince of its good intentions: Japan. Unless it can persuade Japan to accept its new status, Beijing will find leadership in Asia very costly indeed, perhaps even impossible. And yet Beijing has done little to reassure Japan about its future.

And then there is America. China can only lead Asia if America can be persuaded to vacate the field. We have seen that China has grown strong enough to deprive America of primacy in Asia, but it is not yet strong enough to assert primacy itself against American opposition, and has little chance of becoming that strong in future.

All this means that China has little chance of becoming the sole leader of Asia, in either a hard or soft form. Considering the suspicions of Asia's middle powers and the rivalry of its great powers, any bid for outright leadership by China would soon slide into a competition for regional hegemony – a classic 'balance of power' struggle, with potentially huge costs and risks. This lands China in a dilemma. It is now too strong to accept a subordinate role under American leadership, but it is not yet strong enough to lead Asia itself.

Much therefore depends on whether China's leaders come to see this, and whether they can persuade their people of it. We cannot be sure that they will settle for as little as an equal share in the leadership of Asia. We can be sure they will not settle for less. To do so would be to accept a status less than that of a great power. A great power is one strong enough to influence the international system of which it is part to suit its interests. It cannot dictate the shape of the workings of the system, but its views must be taken into account – so no other power can dictate this either. A great power might therefore acknowledge one or more equals in the system – other great powers – but never a superior. The European state system classically included a number of great powers, but Imperial China in its heyday recognised no other great powers in Asia, and under the Monroe Doctrine America has recognised no other great powers in the Western Hemisphere.

In 1972, China tacitly relinquished its claim to great power status in Asia. Today China is strong enough to claim it back, and nothing is more important to China than that claim. If necessary, it will fight for it.

CHAPTER FOUR
THE MILITARY BALANCE

STATUS QUO ANTE

The military balance between America and China is critical to the choices America must make about its role in Asia, but to understand this balance requires more than simply comparing capabilities and budgets. Such comparisons show both how much China's forces have grown and how much larger America's still are, but these two perspectives miss the key point. What matters to their future relationship is not what forces China and America possess, but what they can do with them where and when it counts.

We must look beyond the forces themselves to what they can achieve and what this means for the wider strategic and political relationship. When we do this, we get a rather different sense of US and Chinese relative strengths and weaknesses. We see that while their forces are very different, their military options in relation to one another are surprisingly similar. That means America's bigger and better forces will do little if anything to offset its shrinking advantages in other forms of power, while China's growing military will not be sufficient to allow it to take America's place. China's capacity to limit America's choices in Asia has expanded very markedly over the past decade, but America's capacity to limit China's freedom of action remains formidable.

America's strategic position in Asia has always depended on its strength at sea. Unlike Europe, it has never been a significant land power on the Asian continent, but for over a century it has been the strongest naval power in the Western Pacific, and for much of that time its position has been virtually unchallengeable. It has exercised what naval strategists call 'sea control,' which means it has been able to deploy aircraft carriers and marine amphibious forces throughout the region's oceans with little fear that they would be sunk by an enemy. This 'power projection' capability meant America could quickly bring decisive forces to bear in any conflict on or close to China's coasts, such as over Taiwan. Until the 1990s China had neither the money nor the technology to challenge US sea control and power projection in the Western Pacific, and its strategic priorities lay elsewhere.

Since 1945 America's capability in the Western Pacific has been backed by its nuclear forces. These have generally played a smaller role in America's posture in Asia than they did in Europe during the Cold War, where they compensated for the relative weakness of US conventional forces. That was not necessary in Asia, where US naval and air forces were predominant. Several times in the 1950s, America threatened nuclear attack to coerce China during crises over Laos and the islands of Quemoy and Matsu. This option started to disappear when China built its own nuclear weapons in 1964, and completely vanished when, in the 1970s, China developed missiles that could deliver these weapons to cities in the continental United States. However, China's capacity for nuclear strike on the US continent remained relatively small, and China made no effort to copy the huge arsenals that the Americans and Soviets built during the Cold War. That has made it easy to discount China's nuclear forces as a major factor in the military balance.

THE BALANCE SHIFTS

America's military position in the Western Pacific has not been seriously tested for a long time. US forces have not been in combat in Asia since the end of the Vietnam War, and no crisis has arisen in which combat seemed imminent. In the absence of such tests, it has been easy to take for granted that the United States retains the military means to underwrite its strategic primacy in Asia. But the military balance in Asia began to shift in the 1990s, as China's military priorities changed and its capabilities developed. Three trends drove this. First, China's defence budget grew as its economy grew. Second, the disappearance of the Soviet Union as a major continental threat allowed China to shift priority from land to maritime forces. Third, the willingness of Russia and other parts of the old Soviet Union to sell military technology enabled China to develop its capabilities much faster than would otherwise have been possible. The result has been a surprisingly swift increase in China's air and naval capabilities over the past two decades.[14] The key questions are: what has China been trying to achieve by building this increased maritime capability, and how far has it succeeded? What does this mean for America's ability to maintain primacy?

There are three possible answers to the question of China's intentions. Most ambitiously, it may be aiming for a 'blue-water' naval capability – in other words, the ability to use aircraft carriers, marine forces, long-range submarines and other naval and air forces to project power throughout the Indian and Western Pacific oceans, and perhaps beyond. The most obvious reason it might want to do this is to protect vital seaborne trade, especially oil and gas imports from the Gulf, which seem vulnerable to interdiction by rivals such as America and India. Perhaps it even aspires to acquire enough power to assert political influence far from its shores, as the United States has done and as the Soviets tried to do. Less ambitiously, China might, for the time being at least, be aiming to do these things in the Western Pacific. This would underpin its aspirations to regional leadership in East Asia, but not beyond. Finally, China might be aiming simply to erode America's ability to project power into the Western Pacific, without aiming to develop such a capacity itself.

Some of China's plans – for example, its slow but persistent program to develop aircraft carriers – suggest long-term ambitions to copy America and use naval forces to underpin regional leadership. But if this is the goal, China is still a very long way from it. China is, however, much closer to the most modest of the objectives, and that is in itself highly significant. Simply by limiting America's capacity to project power by sea in the Western Pacific, China is undermining the military foundations of US primacy in Asia and fundamentally challenging Asia's strategic order. And China is already a long way towards achieving this.

The development of China's air and naval forces over the past two decades poses by far the most serious challenge to American sea control in the Western Pacific by an Asian power since the defeat of Japan in 1945. This seems a remarkable state of affairs. Only a few years ago people spoke of America as able to exercise decisive military power anywhere in the world against any adversary with relative ease. That was always exaggerated, as Iraq and Afghanistan have shown. But it also reflected a serious misunderstanding of the nature of military power. America has the largest defence budget, the best technology and the most ships and aircraft. In any even match America would best China every time. But the military contest between them in the Western Pacific is not an even match. It is asymmetrical in several ways, and all of these asymmetries redress the imbalance of forces in China's favour.

First, America is a global power with interests and objectives in many parts of the world, while China is, and will remain for many decades at least, primarily an Asian power. Indeed, it is an *East* Asian power, and its interests are very much focused on its land borders on the Asian continent and the East Asian littoral in the Western Pacific. This means that China's strategic weight is concentrated in this one region, while America's is spread around the globe.

Second, China has the immense advantage that its competition with the United States happens right on its doorstep. American power must be projected across the wide Pacific Ocean and dispersed among widely spaced bases, such as Guam and Okinawa, which for many purposes are poorly located and sometimes politically fragile. This makes a big difference to the cost of maintaining US military operations in the Western Pacific, and means that China can achieve a bigger result for a smaller effort than the United States where it matters most.

Third, and perhaps most importantly, China's primary operational objective is very different from America's, and much simpler and cheaper to achieve. To have primacy in Asia, the United States must preserve the ability to use its carrier and marine forces to back up its diplomacy and, if all else fails, enforce its will in Asia. To accomplish this it must be able to protect those forces from attack at all times – especially at sea. China has a much easier task – not sea control but 'sea denial.' It needs only to be able to attack America's forces where and when it chooses, and thus raise the threat far enough to inhibit US action.

The balance of technological and operational advantage makes sea denial orders of magnitude simpler and cheaper to achieve than sea control. The reason is simple: major warships like aircraft carriers and amphibious assault ships are easier to find and destroy, and much more valuable, than the platforms that can attack them. They are easy to find because they are big and move slowly in two dimensions on the relatively flat and open surface of the sea, and improved sensor technologies have made them even easier to spot in recent decades. Once found, they are relatively easy to attack. Long-range stand-off weapons like anti-ship cruise and ballistic missiles are inherently hard to defend against, especially if they are launched in large numbers. And a high-value target like an aircraft carrier justifies firing enough missiles to saturate defences. Above all, submarines pose a serious threat to ships because they are so hard to detect and their torpedoes are so effective. Although submarines – especially conventionally powered ones – have many critical limitations, the difficulty of detecting them and their ability to threaten ships far from their base make them extremely effective. Perhaps more than any other factor, it is the asymmetry between the stealth of a submarine and the vulnerability of a surface ship that underlies the asymmetry of sea denial and sea control today – an asymmetry that is likely to last for as long as there are no new sensor technologies to deprive submarines of their ability to hide underwater.

Finally, there is a deep asymmetry in the intensity of American and Chinese interest in the Western Pacific. Even in a globalised world, any country's strategic commitments are influenced by geography more than anything else. America's most intense and enduring commitments are concentrated close to home in the Western Hemisphere. In just the same way, China's are concentrated in the Western Pacific and the Asian mainland. That means China has more at stake in Asia than America does. So, all things being equal, China will accept higher risks and costs than America. The closer the two countries' military capabilities converge, the more significant this asymmetry of interest becomes in the final calculations of peace and war, and the more it influences long-term judgements on all sides.

WHAT HAS CHINA ACHIEVED?

Today China is much more capable of finding and sinking American ships than it was fifteen years ago. That has very sharply raised the risks to the United States of sending aircraft carriers and marines to intervene in any crisis involving China. In many situations, deploying extraordinarily valuable ships like aircraft carriers against China in the face of Chinese sea-denial forces is no longer a viable strategic option for Washington.

Much has been written about how China has achieved this, but it is not necessary to revisit it in any detail. The key developments are clear enough. First, China has invested heavily in modern, quiet conventional submarines and is expanding its investment in nuclear-powered attack submarines. These submarines are not as good as US subs, and are perhaps not as well operated, but there are enough of them to pose a very substantial risk to US ships operating anywhere in the East Asian littoral. Second, China has built a large and expanding fleet of fourth-generation Soviet-type combat aircraft. Plane for plane, these will be no match for US aircraft, but operating close to home bases, in defence of China's maritime approaches, their numbers will count for a lot. RAND Corporation studies suggest that it will be very hard for the United States to prevail in an air war over the Taiwan Strait, for example, against the Chinese advantages in location and numbers.[15] Third, China has reportedly developed anti-ship ballistic missiles for use against high-value ships like aircraft carriers that would be very hard to defend against and probably more deadly than conventional cruise missiles. Fourth, China has invested heavily in increasingly robust and effective surveillance, which improves the country's capacity to target US ships, as well as in the ability to neutralise US surveillance and command systems.

All these trends are now well established, and they are very likely to continue for some time. Of course, China has had to learn a lot about how to use the sophisticated technologies it has imported from the countries of the former Soviet Union since the early 1990s, and has even more to learn about how to develop these technologies further on its own. No doubt it still has some way to go, but it would be a mistake to assume that it has not made a great deal of progress in applying and developing its military technology.

As long as its economy keeps growing, China will have the capacity to sustain rapidly growing defence budgets for a long time to come. And as long as the old Russian threat does not revive, China will be able to devote a large share of its defence budget to building up its maritime strength in the Western Pacific. After two decades, in which its defence budget has grown at about 12% per year in real terms, China is still only spending around 2% of GDP on defence, compared with America's 4.7%.[16] China's defence budget is still only about one-fifth the size of America's, but the gap is closing fast. China's costs are lower, and with the advantages of asymmetry noted above, it does not need to spend as much as America to neutralise US advantages and decisively shift the balance of military weight further its way.

The implications of this shift are clear if we compare America's response to the last significant military crisis with China and its future options in a similar situation. In 1996, when China tried to intimidate Taiwanese voters during an election campaign by test-firing missiles into waters close to Taiwan, Washington responded by sailing two aircraft carriers into the area to remind Beijing of America's commitment to Taiwan's security. Beijing took the hint and backed off. In the same situation today, America would have a very different calculation to make. The risk to the carriers would be much higher, and the dangers of escalation more acute. Most probably, Washington would decide to limit its reaction to diplomatic words rather than military deeds. The message received in Beijing would be that much softer, and its effect that much weaker. China's massive investment in air and naval forces will have delivered a significant strategic dividend.

Such dividends have important limits, however. While China has expanded its sea-denial capacity, it is nowhere near achieving sea control itself, even in waters closest to its own homeland. As the great British naval strategist Sir Julian Corbett observed a century ago in another era of shifting power relations, one country can lose sea control without another necessarily acquiring it.[17] China's navy is much more able to sink American ships than ever before, but it has made very little dent in America's countervailing ability to sink Chinese ships. Even with the disadvantages of distance, America's large and very capable forces retain a formidable capacity to prevent China using aircraft carriers or amphibious forces to project power in Asia. If China would now find it relatively easy to locate and sink American carriers, America would have no trouble at all doing the same to any Chinese carriers. Nor for that matter would other large powers such as Japan and India, and even smaller powers such as South Korea, Singapore and Australia. This reflects a critical fact about the strategic environment in Asia over coming decades: the balance of military technology appears to be making it relatively easy to prevent countries from projecting power by sea using big ships like carriers and assault ships. That means we may be entering a 'sea-denial era' in which even the strongest countries will find it hard to project power by sea against another great power, or even against well-equipped middle powers.

This has large implications not just for military power projection, but for the defence of trade as well. It means that China will not be able to defend its seaborne energy imports or other vital supplies from interdiction even in its own immediate approaches, let alone in the distant waters of the Indian Ocean. There is no way China can achieve the sea control needed to protect even a tiny fraction of its vast flow of imports and exports in the face of a campaign by the United States or even a lesser maritime power. But by the same token, it will be relatively easy for China to threaten other countries' trade too, and that means China would be able to defend its own trade by threatening to retaliate against the trade of any attacker – a classic deterrence posture.

What about China's own aircraft carriers? Quite a lot has been made of Beijing's evident determination to acquire these potent symbols of power. China's carrier program seems to show a determination to become a traditional blue-water naval power. Yet Chinese leaders must understand that any of these ships will be as vulnerable to American submarines, or indeed to those of any other great or middle power, as American carriers are to China's. So why would China spend so much money on them? There are three possibilities. First, China's leaders may be making the traditional mistake of putting form ahead of substance in strategic affairs, and building carriers for their prestige and status rather than their operational potential. Second, they may envisage that sometime in the future they will want to project power against smaller countries that lack the capacity to target carriers at sea. Third, they may ambitiously imagine that in the very distant future they may be able to achieve sea control against even major powers such as the United States or Japan, and want to be ready if and when that happens.

While such aspirations give interesting if inconclusive hints about China's long-term plans, our response to China's rise should pay more attention to what it has actually achieved and what it might yet achieve over the next decade or two. In that regard, too much is made of China's ambitions, and not enough of its achievements. From the point of view of China's neighbours in the Western Pacific, the bad news is that China has gone a long way towards limiting America's military reach in Asia. The good news is that it shows no sign of being able to expand its own reach – at least by sea – even as far as its closest island neighbours. On the Asian continent, of course, it is a different story. China's immense population and economy make it a potentially very formidable land power. How China's continental neighbours will deal with this is a fascinating question, but one thing is clear: American conventional forces will play no role. America is not going to fight a continental land war against China in Asia.

HOW CAN AMERICA RESPOND?

Is there anything America can do to restore its military position? Technological breakthroughs might help – for example, a leap forward in submarine detection – but they are unlikely to shift the balance of advantage away from sea denial enough to let the aircraft carriers operate with impunity again. To do that the only option is to destroy as much as possible of China's sea-denial forces before the carriers come within their range. People used to say that the carriers allowed America to project power without going to war. In future America will have to go to war before it can send in the carriers. This means a major campaign of assaults against Chinese submarines and their bases, aircraft and airfields, missile sites and surveillance and command systems. The Pentagon has been putting a lot of work into developing a plan to do just this, looking at how it can maintain America's ability to project power in the face of what it calls Anti-Access and Area-Denial capabilities. China is not the only possible adversary to pose this challenge, but it is overwhelmingly the most important, and clearly the main intended target of the new concept. These plans have been developed in the Air–Sea Battle Concept and the Joint Operational Access Concept.[18] At the operational level, these concepts make reasonable military sense: if the United States is to secure sea control, it must neutralise Chinese sea denial as comprehensively and early as possible.

Strategically, however, the Air–Sea Battle raises very grave questions indeed. As applied to China, the Air–Sea Battle is an operational concept that makes no strategic sense. First, even if the concept was successfully implemented to restore America's ability to project power by sea against China, that would not by itself achieve America's strategic objectives. America would still have to find a way to use the forces it was able to project to win its war against China. On any issue in which China's vital interests are engaged, it is hard to see how this can be done. And for all their formidable power, it is very hard to see how America's conventional forces could compel China to concede defeat. China is not Iraq. America is never going to be able to seize and hold any substantial portion of Chinese territory, or threaten the Chinese government's hold over the country. And how otherwise does it bring any conflict against China to a successful conclusion?

Second, the need to undertake large-scale strikes against a wide range of China's armed forces even before deploying seaborne forces within striking range poses a very high risk of escalation. China would respond with every military option available, and the crisis would swiftly and surely develop into a major war. Any decision to use force against China in the Western Pacific therefore becomes in effect a decision to launch an all-out war. This raises the threshold for intervention a long way. If any substantial intervention requires the United States to undertake a large-scale war against its most important economic partner, then the range of circumstances in which the United States could rationally choose to intervene dwindles accordingly. It becomes unclear whether any US interests in the Western Pacific would justify the costs and risks of defending them on these terms.

The Air–Sea Battle Concept therefore offers no solutions to the strategic implications of China's growing military capabilities. America no longer has the capacity to maintain sea control in the Western Pacific against Chinese naval and air forces, and it has therefore lost the capacity to deploy the sea-based forces that have provided the military foundation for strategic primacy in Asia. This is not a problem that can be washed away with a fire-hose of taxpayers' money. It is true that tight budgets at the

Pentagon over the next few years will make it even harder to respond to China's new capacities, but US fiscal limits have not caused the problem, and spending more money will not make it go away.

How much this matters to America depends on what it is trying to do in Asia. If its objective is to perpetuate the primacy it has exercised until now, then losing sea control to Chinese forces is a major blow. But if America's aim is to play a balancing role, limiting China's capacity to dominate Asia but not seeking to perpetuate its own primacy, then things are not so bad. As we have seen, the United States will be able to deny the Western Pacific to Chinese forces well into the future, and that will remain true no matter how dire the budget squeeze becomes. To dominate China, America needs to maintain sea control; but to balance China, America needs only to maintain sea denial – and it can certainly do that.

THE NUCLEAR DIMENSION

Finally, we have to consider the nuclear dimension. Our thinking about the way nuclear forces play into the relations of major powers has been strongly shaped by the US–Soviet nuclear balance during the Cold War. The US–China nuclear balance looks nothing like this, and that makes it easy to underestimate the role of nuclear weapons in the strategic calculations of each country.

The most obvious difference between the Cold War and today is the asymmetry of forces. China's nuclear forces remain only a small fraction of America's, and its ability to strike targets in the United States itself is tiny compared to Russia's, or to America's ability to strike China. This can make it hard to take China seriously as a nuclear adversary. That would be a very grave mistake. Size alone does not tell the whole story.

The strategic purpose of China's nuclear arsenal has shifted in subtle but important ways over the past decade. Originally its role was minimum deterrence: to provide assurance that China itself would not again – as it had in the 1950s – face nuclear blackmail. To prevent this, China has built up forces sufficient to pose a threat of unacceptable damage to an adversary's homeland in retaliation for any nuclear attack on China. More recently, as China's conventional maritime forces have expanded, the nuclear arsenal has started to take on a wider role. It now also functions to deter the United States from mounting large-scale conventional strikes against China of the sort envisaged by the Air–Sea Battle Concept, by raising the possibility of a Chinese nuclear attack on US bases, such as the one on Guam, from which such strikes would be mounted.

The credibility of this threat hinges on very uncertain calculations on both sides. China would have to calculate that its ability to destroy major American cities would deter the United States from nuclear retaliation against China for a Chinese nuclear attack on Guam. That judgement in turn depends on very uncertain calculations about the scale of strategic interests involved on both sides. During the Cold War, US threats to use nuclear forces to stop a Soviet conventional attack in Europe were credible because it was widely accepted on both sides that America regarded Western Europe as vital to its own security and would be willing to accept devastating nuclear attacks to keep it out of Soviet hands. Would China believe that America's interests in the Western Pacific are likewise important enough to justify accepting nuclear strikes on US cities?

Chinese nuclear strategy presupposes that America's interests in Asia are not as compelling as its interests in Europe were during the Cold War. The Chinese are therefore likely to calculate that the threat of even a relatively minor nuclear strike against US targets would be sufficient to deter large-scale conventional military action against China. It also means that China needs only relatively small nuclear forces to achieve its strategic objectives. And it means that, for China, the nuclear threshold in a conflict with America could be both relatively low and rather uncertain. This works to China's advantage.

All this has important implications for America's allies in Asia as well. Extended nuclear deterrence is central to these alliances. America needs both its allies and China to believe that the United States would launch a nuclear attack on China in retaliation for a nuclear attack on any of its allies, even though it would suffer a Chinese nuclear attack in return. Extended nuclear deterrence therefore only works to the extent that everyone believes that the security of America's allies is as vital to Washington as the security of America itself. The big question will always be whether America can convince China that it will accept a nuclear strike on Los Angeles rather than allow Beijing to take Taiwan. The answer is: probably not.

The temptation for America has been, and remains, to try to solve all these problems at source by being able to deprive China of its nuclear weapons with a disarming first strike. For a long time China's relatively small and vulnerable intercontinental-range nuclear forces has made this a tempting proposition, especially with the prospect that America's modest national missile defence system would be able to destroy any missiles that managed to survive a disarming strike. The possibility that America might be holding open the option of asserting this kind of nuclear primacy over China is reinforced by the careful way in which US official statements about China – unlike those about Russia – avoid acknowledging that China and the United States have a relationship of mutual nuclear deterrence.[19]

But in reality America has no chance of achieving nuclear primacy over China. We can be sure that China will place a very high priority indeed on maintaining its capacity to strike the United States, and that it will succeed in this. It will be much easier for China to expand and protect its long-range missile forces than for America to increase its ability to destroy them, whether on the ground in China or in flight towards the United States. China's ability to impose immense costs on the United States by a nuclear strike on its cities will therefore be a critical factor in the evolution of America's approach to China and the choices it will make about its role in Asia as China's power grows.

Often military issues are discussed quite separately from questions of strategy and politics. Perhaps this is because few people take seriously the possibility of conflict between the United States and China: few see how relatively easy it would be for strategic and political rivalry to slide into military conflict. In fact, as the United States and China compete for power in Asia, the possibility of conflict is very real, and the more intensely they compete, the more likely conflict becomes. Moreover, judgements about who would prevail if the two sides fight, and at what cost, influence the actions and reactions of Washington and Beijing, and of all the other players in Asia, even when conflict itself seems remote. So these shifts in the military balance between the two countries in Asia are critical in assessing American choices about how to respond to China.

CHAPTER FIVE
THE ASIAN SETTING

ASIAN CHOICES

America does not face China alone. It has both longstanding allies and important new friends in Asia who look to Washington for reassurance that China's rise will not come at their expense. All of them have flourished under US primacy in the decades since Vietnam, and all hope America will prevent China dominating the region and misusing its power at their expense. They are a formidable group. The allies include Japan, South Korea, Australia, the Philippines and Thailand, and the friends include India, Indonesia, Singapore and Vietnam. Their support could be a major asset to America in responding to China's power. But the essential question to consider is not whether China's neighbours will support America's presence in Asia, but whether they will support its primacy.

Every country in Asia today faces its own choices about China, and those choices are complex as well as momentous. They do not face a simple decision between supporting China or supporting America, any more than America faces a simple decision between maintaining primacy in Asia or abandoning the region to Chinese hegemony. It is important to see this. If China's Asian neighbours were forced to choose between US primacy and Chinese hegemony, Washington could be sure of their strong support, because no one in Asia wants to live under China's thumb. That leads many people who believe that there is no third option for Asia between US primacy and Chinese hegemony to assume that the rest of Asia will support America unquestioningly and unreservedly. It also leads them to believe that, in return, America has no choice but to support them against China at almost any cost. Both beliefs are wrong.

Partly these mistakes arise because of the lingering genie of the North Atlantic Treaty Organization (NATO). The central role of NATO in the Cold War has left America with a deep attachment to this model of US leadership, and a tendency to exaggerate its value in other circumstances. Policymakers start to see maintaining America's alliances as a primary interest in its own right, rather than as a means to serve other, more fundamental purposes. As America addresses China's challenge, and despite disavowals that it seeks to contain China as it contained the Soviets, it is perhaps inevitable that it implicitly turns to NATO as a model for an Asian coalition. But China is very different from the Soviet Union. It poses a different kind of challenge to American power, and America's interests are different too. These differences make the NATO model hard to apply in Asia over the next few decades.

In reality, China's neighbours in Asia do not face a simple binary choice between two stark visions of their future. They face the need to strike a complex and shifting balance between conflicting imperatives. Certainly none of them wants to live under China's thumb, but equally none of them wants to make China an enemy. Above all, they want peace, stability and opportunities to grow. They will choose whatever course best provides these things, and that will depend on the choices that America and China both make. The more determined China seems to dominate Asia, and to that end tries to exclude America altogether from the region, the more its neighbours will be inclined to support the United States in pushing back. But the more willing China is to accept limits to its power and work with America in a new regional order, the more comfortable its neighbours will be to see it play a larger role. Similarly, the more determined America seems to perpetuate its primacy in Asia, and to that end seeks to escalate rivalry and risk war rather than accommodate China's aspirations for greater influence, the less support America will receive from China's neighbours. Asian countries will support America to resist Chinese hegemony, but not to deny China a larger role in Asian affairs. They will accommodate a modestly ambitious China, but will not appease a hegemonic one.

This suggests that Asia's strategic alignments over the next few decades are going to be much more complicated than a simple 'with us or against us.' Every country in Asia must balance deep anxieties about China's growing power and ambition against strong imperatives to get along with Beijing. Unlike America's Cold War allies against the Soviets, they have much to gain from China economically, and little to fear politically. All of them expect China to be central to their own economies. None of them worry that Chinese ideology will subvert their people and undermine their political systems, as America's allies in the Cold War did. All are aware of how vulnerable they might be in a major regional war against China, and how much they might suffer if intense competition becomes entrenched.

Moreover, they do not share America's interest in American primacy for its own sake. The communiqués might talk of shared values, but America's allies in Asia are practical folk for whom such talk means little against the overriding imperative for peace and order. For them, American primacy has no intrinsic value. They have welcomed and supported it for the last forty years only because it has been the foundation of peace and stability in Asia. They will continue to support it as long as that remains true, but not otherwise. They will not sacrifice their interests in peace and stability, and good relations with China, to support US primacy unless that is the only way to avoid Chinese domination.

Their confidence in America's commitment to their security will also dwindle as power shifts. Asian governments understand that as China's power grows, it becomes both a more valuable economic partner to the United States and a more formidable strategic adversary. They will realistically recognise that for both these reasons the costs to America of supporting an Asian ally against China will rise, and the threshold for American intervention will therefore rise too. They will increasingly fear that they risk being entrapped in America's conflicts with China and abandoned by America in their own. America, of course, will have the same concerns about them. Building and maintaining a coalition to resist China's challenge to American primacy will therefore become increasingly difficult for all sides. We can best understand these difficulties, and the important opportunities that still exist for the United States to work with Asian friends and allies, by looking at the more important of them in more detail.

GREAT POWERS
JAPAN
Japan is the Asian power that will be most willing to support the United States in maintaining its supremacy. This matters, because

Japan is by far America's most important ally in Asia. It is a remarkable and perhaps unique relationship. For decades the world's second-richest country has remained a strategic client of the world's richest country – one great power as the client of another. This is surely unprecedented, and reflects rather special, and perhaps transitory, conditions. The relationship has been vital to America's position in Asia, but it rests on unstable foundations, because it puts Japan in a predicament that becomes more and more untenable the stronger China grows.

Japan's predicament is this: it deeply fears China's growing power, believing that the stronger China becomes, the more it will constrain Japan politically and economically. Japan's leaders have little faith that China will prove a benign regional leader, allowing Japan the space to develop and prosper in its own way. Partly, of course, this is because of the two countries' difficult history, but more fundamentally it is because Japan itself is inherently a great power in the Asian system.

That claim might seem surprising. After two decades of stagnation Japan is no longer the economic powerhouse it was in the 1980s, and its economic trajectory over the next few decades hardly looks to improve. But it remains the world's third-largest economy, with immense industrial and technological resources, great social cohesion, a deep sense of its unique identity, and the strategic advantages of insular territory. It will never again be a land power on the Asian continent, as it was for half a century before 1945. But it can easily build formidable maritime and nuclear forces that would give it a decisive place in Asia's strategic balance. If a great power is one strong enough to disrupt any regional order that does not satisfy it, then Japan will have the capacity to be a great power in Asia for many decades to come. This is a problem for China. Just as American leadership in the

Western Hemisphere has depended on there being no great powers to compete with it, so China's ambitions for regional leadership cannot tolerate Japan as an independent great power. If China is to lead Asia, Japan must relinquish its great power potential and accept the subordinate status of a middle power. So Japan is right to be worried about China's rise.

As long as Japan's alliance with America remains the centrepiece of its strategic policy, it will depend almost completely on Washington to protect it from Chinese pressure. The problem is that the more powerful China becomes, the less Japan can depend on the United States. As China grows, it increasingly becomes both too valuable a partner and too threatening an adversary for America to be willing always to sacrifice its interests in a good relationship with China to support Japan. The risk of abandonment by Washington will grow if the United States and China reach an understanding about their respective roles in Asia, which Washington would be reluctant to jeopardise on Japan's behalf. In other words, the better the United States and China get on, the less secure Japan feels, and conversely, the worse the US–China relations become, the more confident Japan will be about America's support. This puts Japan in the untenable situation of relying for its security on an adversarial relationship between its two most important international partners. Escalating rivalry between Washington and Beijing would be disastrous for Japan, but so too would friendship and cooperation.

The only clear way for Japan to get out of this predicament is to stop relying on America for protection from China. Instead it would have to build forces of its own capable of resisting Chinese pressure. That would almost certainly mean building nuclear forces sufficient to provide a minimum deterrent against Chinese nuclear attack, so that Japan could not be subject to

Chinese nuclear blackmail. This would obviously be an immensely difficult decision for any Japanese government, but it is not unthinkable and the alternatives are very dire.

Such a step would mark a fundamental change in Japan's international position. It would mean its re-emergence as an independent great power and spell the end of its alliance with the United States. At first glance it seems that this would be a huge blow to America's position in Asia, but the closer we look, the less clear that becomes. As China grows, the alliance with Japan could become a significant liability for Washington in two ways. First, it entangles America in Japan's disputes with China. There is a growing risk that America will be drawn into conflict with China over a dispute between Tokyo and Beijing in which America has no direct stake, simply to preserve the credibility of its security undertakings to Japan. Second, Japan's anxiety about America becoming too close to China means that the need to preserve the credibility of the alliance inhibits Washington from seeking a durable settlement with Beijing. Maintaining the alliance with Japan might therefore preclude a stable and peaceful US relationship with China. Whether it is worth that cost depends on America's ultimate aims in Asia. If it is determined to perpetuate its strategic primacy, then preserving the alliance with Japan is essential and the consequences for relations with China must be accepted. But if, as I will argue, America can maintain a strong position in the Western Pacific and protect its core interests without maintaining primacy, then the Japan alliance will cost the United States more than it is worth.

INDIA

Since the 1990s, American policymakers have looked to India as a counterweight to China. They hope that as India's power grows, it will augment American power to offset China's rise and help preserve the US-led order. The strategic relationship has come a long way over the last decade, with increased cooperation on many levels.

Nevertheless, it is easy to exaggerate what it all amounts to. It is not in any sense an alliance. Washington can have no expectations of substantial support from Delhi in the event of a clash with China, except insofar as it serves India's direct interests. There is no reason, for example, to expect India to send forces to support the United States in a confrontation with China over Taiwan or in the South China Sea.

Some people hope that a genuine alliance will evolve in future, but there are three reasons to doubt this. Like America, India will increasingly see China as its principal strategic competitor, but India's objectives in relation to China will not be the same as America's. Indeed, as India grows stronger, its interests are likely to diverge further and further from America's, especially if America's aim is to maintain primacy in Asia. As India emerges as a great power in its own right, with an intense sense of its place in the world, its aim will be to maximise its own power, not support America's. India will be happy to work with America to limit China's power and prevent China becoming dominant, but will not subordinate its own ambitions for leadership in favour of America's. Looking further ahead, the stronger India becomes, the less it will need America to help balance China, and the more it will want to use its strength to enhance its own power, not America's. Equally, and conversely, the stronger China is relative to India, the more cautious Delhi will be about sacrificing its interest in a good relationship with Beijing to protect America's position in Asia rather than promote its own. So even if India becomes a formidable great power in the Asian

Century, it will be a relatively modest support for American primacy.

This does not make India a strategic liability for America in the way Japan might be, because India's relationship with America is not as important as Japan's and its relationship with China is not as toxic. But it does mean that India will be an asset to America in confronting China only to the extent that America's aims match India's interests. And India's interests do not require American primacy, so if that is America's aim, India will not be much help.

RUSSIA

Arguably, Russia is a third great power in Asia that might help America to manage China, but its role in the power politics of the Asian Century is hard to predict. The first uncertainty is how strong Russia will be. It remains a country with immense territory, resources and – notwithstanding serious demographic pressures – a large, highly educated and very capable population. Nonetheless, its economy is narrow and fragile, and nothing suggests that it is building the economic weight to be a great power in Asia over coming decades. Like Japan, Russia will probably be on the defensive against China for a long time to come, but unlike Japan it must defend a long land border against China's army, which will become a harder and harder task as China's power grows.

Of course Russia will always – or at least for a long time – have a lot of nuclear weapons. They will help Russia to defend against existential threats where the danger of nuclear strike is credible. But they will be no substitute for conventional forces able to meet conventional attacks by China against Russia's Far East, because it will be hard for Russia to credibly threaten nuclear strikes, with the high risk of Chinese nuclear retaliation against core Russian cities, to defend distant territory on the margins of the Russian empire. So unless Moscow is willing and able to spend enough to build massive land forces in its Far East, its strategic position in Asia is likely to become increasingly tenuous.

How much will this matter to Moscow? Clearly Siberia is critical both to Russia's economy and its identity, but Russian interests and emotions are much more intensely engaged to its west and south than to its east. Russia has not lost territory in the Far East, whereas in the west it has lost huge territories that are economically, culturally and strategically critical. If Russia grows stronger in future, its attention will turn first to the lost lands of its near-abroad in Europe, where the potential for Russia to reverse the post-Soviet dissolution of the Russian empire remains the principal danger to the European order. So Russia is unlikely to devote much effort to the Far East, and may even be willing to retrench there if necessary to focus its energies in the west.

Of course Russia will not be indifferent to China's rise. But its vulnerability to Chinese land power suggests that it will be unwilling to support a coalition to resist the Chinese challenge to US primacy. In fact, its interests in Europe may make it happy to see American attention diverted elsewhere. Only if China seemed likely to succeed in dominating Asia would Russia be willing to shift its attention from the west – and by then it would quite probably be too late. In other words, even if its economy rebounds and it becomes a great power in Europe again, Russia seems unlikely to regain its status as great power in Asia, and in the longer term its hold on the Russian Far East may prove untenable.

MIDDLE POWERS
SOUTH KOREA

South Korea is America's most important ally among Asia's middle powers. Washington's role in helping Seoul meet the threat from North Korea makes the alliance look very durable. North Korea's nuclear capability seems only to strengthen it further, because America's nuclear forces are all that protects Seoul from Pyongyang's nuclear blackmail. Yet if we look a little closer, it is not clear how valuable the alliance will be either to South Korea or to the United States in the future.

Consider South Korea's perspective first. For Seoul, the US alliance has three primary targets: China, North Korea and Japan. The most pressing of these is North Korea. How useful is the US alliance going to be in managing this threat? That depends partly, of course, on what happens north of the demilitarised zone. Predicting the future of the North Korean regime is risky: its fundamental weakness is clear, but so too is its quirky capacity to survive. It may collapse at any time or it may last for decades, so we should consider both scenarios.

If the North collapses, Seoul's overriding priority will be to reunify the two Koreas under South Korea's political and economic system. China will have by far the biggest say over whether and how this happens, as it has by far the largest capacity to intervene in North Korea with political support, economic aid, emergency relief and armed force. It could keep North Korea running in some form as a separate state if it chose, and would therefore have the power to decide whether or not the North is absorbed by the South. By contrast, America's influence on events in North Korea will be negligible. This means that if the North collapses, Seoul will need Beijing's help much more than America's, giving Beijing the power to set conditions for reunification. For example, China might easily demand as the price for this that the US–South Korea alliance be dissolved and all American forces leave the Peninsula. How likely is it that Seoul would refuse? Why should it, if the North Korean threat had disappeared?

If the North survives, and especially if new leaders in Pyongyang follow China's economic example, then South Korea will face a different problem. As long as North Korea remains a threat to the South, the question for Seoul will be: which of Asia's great powers can do more to help keep the North at bay? At first glance the answer might seem to be America, but a closer look suggests it is more likely to be China. The North Korean provocations against the South in 2010 tell an interesting story about why this should be so. When the North sunk the *Cheonan* and shelled South Korean territory, the United States strongly backed Seoul and promised firm responses to future provocations, while China refused to condemn the North and was apparently unable to constrain it. The first impression, therefore, was that America had shown its strength and value as an ally to Seoul, while China was either unable or unwilling to help.

However, first impressions can mislead. When we look ahead the picture changes, and the relative positions of the United States and China seem to shift. Think first about what the United States can do next time North Korea stages a provocation against the South. Washington has promised a robust response, but it lacks credible military options. The United States could launch retaliatory strikes against North Korea, or support the South to do so, but it could not be sure that North Korea would not respond in turn, leading to a risky cycle of escalation which the United States could not control. Essentially,

Washington can do little to help Seoul deal with Pyongyang because the only means of influence it has over the North is military coercion, to which Pyongyang can respond in kind. Beijing, by contrast, has many more effective ways to influence North Korea, and thus is potentially more useful to Seoul than Washington might be. It may well be that Beijing's refusal to lean on Pyongyang in 2010 was an unsubtle way of reminding Seoul of this. If Seoul chooses to lean towards Washington, the message seems to have been, they should not expect Beijing to help them manage the North. Seoul might well conclude that a close relationship with Beijing is better insurance against the North than the alliance with Washington.

What about the relationship with China itself? There is no doubt that South Korea, like other Asian countries, values America's support in dealing with China. But how far can Seoul rely on America against China? As with Japan, Seoul's confidence in US support depends on a judgement about the extent to which the United States will in future value its relations with South Korea higher than its relations with China. The stronger China becomes, the less confident Seoul can be about this, because America will be increasingly unlikely to jeopardise vital economic relations or risk a major conflict with China to protect purely Korean interests. Indeed, Korea could only have confidence in US support against China if that was clearly in American interests, which would mean if the United States and China were already locked in rivalry. Whether supporting the United States in an intense strategic competition with China would be in Seoul's interests would depend on how threatening China appeared, but unless China becomes aggressively hegemonist, South Koreans might easily decide that they would be better off staying neutral rather than siding with America.

And Japan? How far Seoul could rely on Washington for support against Tokyo would depend on the state of the US–Japan
relationship. If Japan and South Korea both remain US allies,
then that support seems secure. But Seoul must be sensitive to
the possibility that if Washington is compelled to choose one side
or the other, it would be likely to go with Japan, simply because
Japan is a more powerful state and ally. And if Japan ceases to be a
US ally, then Seoul could have less confidence that Washington
would be willing or able to do much to support South Korea
against Japan. In fact, if it is Japan that the Koreans are worried
about, Beijing would clearly be a better ally than Washington.

So much for the Korean perspective. How does the alliance
look from America's end? Considered carefully, the costs and
risks of this alliance are quite high. Apart from the large cost of
major deployments in South Korea, the alliance carries a significant risk of conflict with North Korea. It also carries a lower but
still serious risk of drawing America into conflict with either
China or Japan, if South Korea sought American help in a confrontation with either of its large neighbours. And what are the
offsetting benefits? For the reasons sketched above, Seoul will not
risk serious rupture with Beijing to support the United States
against China, unless China becomes overtly aggressive towards
it. If, as is more likely, China tries to reassure Seoul, America will
find it hard to persuade Seoul to turn its back. As we have seen,
China simply has too many cards to play on issues that matter to
Seoul for it to be willing to break with China in any but the most
extreme circumstances.

Essentially, like China's other Asian neighbours, South Korea
has a big interest in the United States staying in Asia to balance
China, but it has much less interest in sacrificing its relationship
with China in order to support an American bid to maintain

primacy in Asia. American primacy is not that important to South Korea, and China is very important indeed.

SOUTHEAST ASIA

Southeast Asia appears to offer America many opportunities to garner support for maintaining primacy in Asia. The United States has two allies there – Thailand and the Philippines – and growing connections with several other substantial middle powers: Indonesia, Vietnam and Singapore, in particular. American policymakers appear to hope that these relationships can be deepened and strengthened over coming years, as Southeast Asian countries become more anxious about China's power and more willing to look to America for protection, and more willing to support America in return.

China has helped in this: after several years of quite effective diplomatic cultivation designed to reassure its Southeast Asian neighbours about its intentions towards them, China has recently become more high-handed and intimidating. Naturally, the Southeast Asians have looked to America for support. But even so, America's strategic relationships in Southeast Asia remain very weak. There are no clear commitments to support the United States against China, and such commitments are unlikely to develop unless driven by overt Chinese aggression. Meanwhile, America's increasingly explicit commitments to these countries risk entangling it in their disputes with China.

Take Vietnam as an example. China has become increasingly assertive in pressing its claims against Vietnam to disputed islands and waters in the South China Sea. America has been happy to express support for Vietnam in response. American policymakers clearly hope that this will lay the foundations for a long-term alignment of Washington and Hanoi, and substantial

Vietnamese support for American efforts to resist China's challenge. But how realistic is this? Vietnam has a huge stake, economically and strategically, in good relations with China. As long as it has any hope of sustaining that relationship, it will not risk it by supporting the United States against China over any issues in which its own interests are not very directly engaged. Again, apply the Taiwan test: would Vietnam support the United States against China in a crisis over Taiwan? If not, what real strategic benefit does America gain from a closer engagement with Vietnam? On the other hand, the costs are potentially very high. By voicing its support for Vietnam over the South China Sea, America runs a serious risk of being drawn into a crisis between China and Vietnam. US statements in recent years have given rise to an expectation that if a future clash escalates to an exchange of fire, America will offer Vietnam concrete support. If it doesn't, the credibility of its claims to the lead role in Asian security is seriously damaged. If it does, relations with China plummet. It is far from clear that America's interests in the Spratly Islands are worth a war with China.

The same could be said of any of the other Southeast Asian powers. All of them want America to stay engaged in Asia to balance China's power. But all of them have an equally strong interest in good relations with China, and will not sacrifice that interest to offer the United States substantial support against China – unless they are directly threatened themselves. And all of them threaten to entangle the United States in their own quarrels with Beijing.

TAIWAN

Finally, of course, there is Taiwan. Taiwan remains the most difficult specific issue of all. Both sides have been willing to manage this issue to avoid disruption to the wider relationship, but it remains the point on which American and Chinese views of their positions and prerogatives in Asia are most clearly incompatible. That is because, over the past forty years, Taiwan's status has been veiled in a deeply destabilising ambiguity. It is acknowledged by every significant player to be part of China, but it is also accorded some of the most critical qualities of an independent state. By proclaiming a One China policy, we all tell Beijing that we regard Taiwan as part of China, but we deny China the right to treat it as such. This anomaly is not the product of high policy principles alone. It is as much the result of a political fix to defuse and deflect awkward opposition in Washington to the development of relations with China after 1972. We live today with the legacy of that fix: an unresolved anomaly in the fabric of the international relations of Asia. The reason this anomaly remains so dangerous is that both the United States and China have come to see the status of Taiwan – or rather, the actions of the other in relation to Taiwan – as a critical index of their respective places in Asia's power structure. For China the right to use force to reclaim what it sees as a wayward province is potent proof of its return to great power status in Asia. For America its ability to prevent that is equally potent proof of its continuing status as the primary power in Asia and the arbiter of regional affairs.

As long as the status quo can be sustained, these ambiguities can remain unresolved. Both Washington and Beijing have been content to leave it that way. It has become easy to believe that the issue will somehow go away. Yet this seems too optimistic. There are two ways in which the issue could come to a head. First, the status quo depends on Taiwan's politics. A future Taiwanese leader could quite easily trigger a US–China confrontation by taking a step towards independence that to Beijing requires a forceful response. That risk has seemed to fade with the swing from the more assertive polices of President Chen to the more accommodating President Ma, but it would be rash to assume the swing could not be reversed. Second, the temperature of the Taiwan issue between Washington and Beijing depends in part on the tone of the broader relationship. If rivalry intensifies, Taiwan could easily become a strategic football again.

America's choices about China therefore require some choices about Taiwan too. They will not be easy. Let us first sketch the underlying power dynamics. They are moving relentlessly China's way. America's commitment to defend Taiwan started losing credibility once China could launch a nuclear strike on the American homeland, and it has become less and less credible the more China's power – both military and economic – has grown. Today no American leader could ignore the almost unimaginable economic costs of a conflict with China over Taiwan. Nor could they ignore the growing risks to US operations in the Western Pacific from Chinese forces. Most sobering of all, no American leader could dismiss the risk that a conflict over Taiwan would escalate to a nuclear exchange involving devastating strikes on US cities.

So the United States faces a stark choice: does it regard Taiwan's current status as so central to the international order that it would run the risk of war with China to preserve it? And how exactly would such a conflict end – would America have a way to end hostilities on terms that left the people of Taiwan any better off? The answers to these questions carry an important message. The United States can no longer prevent China seizing Taiwan by force. A major war between them would cost the

United States far more than Taiwan's status could possibly be worth, and would leave the Taiwanese far worse off than they would be as a result of forced reunification with China. This judgement does not underestimate the terrible consequences of forced reunification. It simply balances them against a sober assessment of the much more terrible consequences of major, quite probably nuclear, war.

If this is right, then America can no longer defend Taiwan from China, and a policy towards Taiwan that presumes that it can is unsustainable. What kind of policy might replace it? The first step is to clarify what US interests are, and how they would be affected by different outcomes. Strategically, it is hard to see that reunification harms US interests. Possession of Taiwan by China would not make any real difference to the strategic balance between the United States and China in the Western Pacific. Politically, too, America has no direct interest in whether Taiwan merges into China or remains separate, so long as reunification takes place without compulsion. The United States, therefore, has no reason to oppose reunification if it happens with the unforced consent of a majority of Taiwanese people. Many believe that this is exactly where things are headed, as economic and social links grow across the Strait. Clearly this is what Beijing hopes will happen too. America today, however, remains at least implicitly opposed to this outcome. It will not express support for reunification, no matter how peacefully it happens. This is not in America's interest, nor is it in the interest of the people of Taiwan. There is no reason for the United States to oppose eventual, peaceful, consensual reunification of Taiwan with China, and every reason to encourage it.

CHAPTER SIX
AMERICA'S OPTIONS, AMERICA'S OBJECTIVES

AMERICA'S OPTIONS

We have examined the setting in which America faces the need to make major choices about China. We now turn to the choice itself. There are essentially just three ways in which America can respond to China's challenge to its leadership in Asia. First, it can concede the field to China and withdraw from any major role in Asian affairs. Second, it can resist China's challenge and try to maintain its position of primacy. Third, it can stay in Asia but fashion a new role for itself within a new order, in which it shares power with China.

Although American leaders may try to blur the issue, politics and public opinion on both sides of the Pacific will ensure that ultimately a clear choice will have to be made to take one of these three very different paths. In America, people will want to know whether their country still leads in Asia or not, and why, and what commitments and responsibilities they incur as a result. In China, they will want to be clear on whether their country is now acknowledged as a leader or still treated as a follower, and will look for either palpable signs of its new status or determined efforts to win it. America's friends and allies will need to know whether America still claims a leading role in Asia, and if so what that role is and what it means for them. These questions cannot be obfuscated indefinitely. Sooner or later, America's actions will make its choice clear, even if its leaders' words do not. Our central question, then, is which of these three options should America choose? To answer this question, we must first ask: what would each option mean for America, and for Asia?

WITHDRAW

At first glance America seems very unlikely to respond to China's rise by pulling back. As America's leaders so often say, their country has been a major power in Asia for over a century, and its interests there are as compelling today as they have ever been. Indeed, as Asia moves more and more to the centre of world affairs, America seems to have stronger reasons than ever to remain an Asian power. However, America is an Asian power by choice, and in the long run it will choose to stay for only as long as it believes the benefits of that choice outweigh the costs. For a long time, and especially since 1972, the balance has been overwhelmingly positive: uncontested primacy in Asia has cost America relatively little while delivering huge benefits. When American political leaders and policy analysts say that America will always remain an Asian power, they tend to assume that the balance will always stay positive.

This was a fair assumption as long as America remained Asia's unchallenged leader, but the stronger China becomes, the more it will cost America to maintain its position against Chinese pressure. It will need to deploy more forces in Asia and do more to support friends and allies. If staying in Asia means accepting either the economic costs and strategic risks of rivalry with China or the political costs of sharing power with it – and those are the only alternatives – then withdrawal might start to seem to many Americans a serious and attractive option.

What would American withdrawal mean? In Beijing they would no doubt hope and expect that China would at last have the chance to fulfil its aspirations and take America's place at the apex of the Asian order. Much would depend on how China used its power, and how other Asian countries responded to it. If China was content to exercise leadership with a light hand – the Monroe Doctrine model – and its neighbours were willing to accept its leadership, then the region might muddle along reasonably well without America. But it seems much more likely that China's bid for leadership would be fiercely resisted, especially by stronger powers such as Japan and India, and especially if China's leadership turned out to be harsh and oppressive. Asia would then face a dark future riven by conflict among its great powers.

US withdrawal from Asia would therefore most likely lead not to Chinese hegemony but to a protracted bitter struggle between China and its neighbours, as China tried and failed to establish primacy over them. As we have seen, for all its strength China is not strong enough to dominate Asia if the other major powers choose to resist. Asia would soon become divided into competing camps in a classic balance-of-power system, punctuated by serious wars. It is hard to see a stable and peaceful future for Asia without a strong US presence of some kind.

COMPETE

America's most natural and instinctive response to China's challenge is to push back. It is not just that primacy in the world's most vibrant region has served America's strategic and economic interests well. It also fits America's image of itself much better than either of the other options. This makes competing with China for leadership in Asia the default option for America. But where would it lead? There seem three possible outcomes.

The first is that, sooner or later, China concedes defeat and decides to accept US leadership again. This is presumably what people who advocate a contest with China expect to happen. They assume that China will cave in quickly, without America having to exert itself too much, and certainly without any major military conflict or economic disruption. That is not impossible, but it is a long, long way from being probable. Three scenarios are worth considering. One is that China, as it is today, will simply call off the challenge. This scenario assumes that China's challenge is not really serious, and that Beijing will soon wake up and realise that it has neither the means nor the motive to contest America's position in Asia. As we saw in Chapter Three, this is implausible. It would be unwise for America to commit to escalating competition with a country as powerful as China on a slender hope that it isn't serious. Wiser to assume that China today is determined to contest US leadership in Asia in order to restore the status of a great power that it is sure it deserves and believes it can achieve.

The second scenario is that China's political system will change fundamentally as it grows, and that sometime in the future it will reach the point where it decides that an international order based on American primacy is the best bet after all.[20] Again, this is not impossible, but it is hardly very likely. It assumes that China will change politically and ideologically, which, as we have seen, is far from assured: if it continues to adapt and deliver, China's one-party system could last a long time yet. It also assumes that political and ideological differences are driving China's challenge to America. It is much more likely that simple nationalism is the main driver of Chinese ambitions, and that is unlikely to disappear even if China does undergo radical political change. Finally, this scenario overlooks the effect of America's own actions on Chinese attitudes. The more America tries to force China to accept US primacy, the less likely it is that China will do so. If we really believe that China will change over time and come to accept American primacy, the best policy will be to stand back and give it plenty of space, because that will make it easier to persuade the Chinese that US primacy is in their interests too.

The third scenario is that China will be compelled by US pressure to abandon its challenge. How likely is this? It depends partly on the balance of strength between them, and partly on the balance of will. How hard can America push, and how hard can China push back? How does America's willingness to pay the costs match up against China's determination to become, and be treated as, a great power? No one can be sure, but the most likely answers are that the two powers are equally matched in their capacity to apply pressure to the other, but that China has a clear edge on determination. They are equally matched on power because, while America can apply more political and diplomatic clout than China, China can apply more financial and economic pressure, and as we have seen, America's apparent advantages in military power and regional support turn out to be rather weaker than they seem. China is probably more determined because the issues go to more fundamental questions of its international status. America can relinquish primacy in Asia without abandoning its place as a great power in Asia, but if China accepts American primacy in Asia it must abandon its claims to being a great power there or anywhere else. And for China, Asia is home. Just as America will always care more about its role in the Western Hemisphere than China does, the stakes for China in Asia will always, in the end, be higher than for America. All this suggests that it would be unwise to embark on a policy of forcing China to accept US primacy unless America was willing to settle in for a long and very costly struggle.

So China is unlikely to concede defeat and decide to resume its subordinate role. The second possible outcome of an American decision to compete with China is that the United States sooner or later concedes defeat after finding that the costs and risks involved are more than it is willing to bear. This seems very unlikely. Once the United States unambiguously commits to rivalry with China, conceding defeat would be almost unthinkable. Avoiding this would soon become more important even than the original objective, and the pressure would be huge, not to withdraw, but to escalate in the hope that China would cave in first.

We can see where this leads. If America decides to maintain primacy in Asia against China's opposition, the most likely outcome is an escalating and open-ended strategic competition between the world's two strongest states. If China does not abandon its challenge, it will respond to America's push-back with a push-back of its own, forcing America either to concede or escalate in turn. It is much less likely that America would concede. So, in the words of General David Petraeus: tell me how this ends?

SHARE

The third option for America is to try to find a way to share power with China in Asia. That would mean negotiating a new distribution of political authority and influence to more closely match the new distribution of power. America's aim would be to maximise its authority and influence in Asia, and to minimise China's, consistent with avoiding an escalating conflict. This means agreeing on a distribution of influence between them that concedes China the minimum with which it would be satisfied. For both sides, reaching that agreement would be very hard, both diplomatically and politically. For America, sharing power with China would mean diluting a great deal of its political authority and influence in Asia. But we can be pretty sure that China would not settle for anything less than full equality with the United States in a shared regional leadership. To have any chance of success, the United States would have to be prepared to treat China as an equal. This would not be easy. How it might work is explored in detail in later chapters.

AMERICA'S OBJECTIVES

America faces a hard task in choosing among these three options. The first challenge is to recognise fundamental long-term aims. Over time these can easily be confused with the means used to achieve them – in other words, we may mistake preserving the means for attaining the ends. America's leadership in Asia, and the military forces, alliances and understandings that support it, have worked so well for so long that they have come to seem ends in themselves, rather than means to the primary objective. So it is important to consider carefully what ultimately matters to America in Asia. Why has primacy there been important? What are the ultimate national purposes that it is intended to serve? Is it still the best way to achieve these purposes? And might other approaches to Asia serve those purposes as well, or better?

At first glance America's reasons for being in Asia seem clear enough. The familiar sentences have been used so often that they have become smooth and slippery with use. Asia is home to some of America's oldest and closest allies. Many Americans trace their origins to Asia. America has been an Asian power for over a century. Above all, as the world's most dynamic region, Asia is increasingly vital to America's economy. All these statements are true, and they have been enough to remind Americans why they were right not to step back from leadership in Asia after the Cold War. But now America faces more complex choices, and we need to dig deeper. The question now is not simply whether to stay in the region or abandon it, but about the *form* of American engagement. To make these more nuanced judgements, we need a more precise idea of why Asia matters to America, and how much it matters. I think we can best do this by bringing the discussion back to the three basic needs of people and nations alike: prosperity, security and identity.

PROSPERITY

America's most obvious objective in Asia is to continue to benefit from the world's economic powerhouse, as a source of imports, a market for exports, a place to invest and a source of capital. This has two aspects: first, America needs Asia's economy to remain vibrant and growing; and second, it needs it to remain open to American businesses. These are connected, but not identical, and they are worth looking at separately.

First, for Asia to keep growing it must remain peaceful and stable, so America has a big economic interest in Asia's security. For the past forty years, as we have seen, Asia has been peaceful because of American primacy, and the link between them has been clear. Now we are entering a new era in which that link may no longer hold. Maintaining US primacy may no longer be the best way to keep Asia peaceful. If maintaining primacy means competing for it against China, this will undermine Asian security and slow or reverse Asian economic growth, which in turn will hit America's economy hard. Over the next few years, America could easily find that a policy of maintaining regional primacy actually damages its economic interests. On the other hand, withdrawal could carry the same risk. Without a strong US presence, the region's other major powers will most likely fall into a cycle of destabilising rivalry among themselves, with equally grave economic consequences. This suggests that the best way to support American economic interests in Asia is neither to withdraw nor to compete for primacy.

Second, America's economic future depends not only on Asia's continued dynamism, but also on American access to its markets. In recent decades, the United States has been the prime mover when it comes to economic openness and integration. But such openness is now to everyone's long-term advantage; for a long time to come China and the other Asian economies are likely to be clear beneficiaries of it, so they will not need American leadership to keep them committed. Indeed, protectionist pressures are more likely to come from America. Or else the most serious threat to trade across the Pacific might be strategic rivalry between the United States and China which then spills over into the economic sphere. This would start to affect trade and investment decisions on both sides of the Pacific. Hence the greatest threat to US economic opportunities in Asia might arise from the American determination to retain primacy.

SECURITY

Prosperity is one objective, security another. For almost a century, US strategy outside the Western Hemisphere has had a single underlying aim. America has been determined to prevent the emergence of a power on the Eurasian continent strong enough to project power across America's ocean approaches and threaten the security of the continental United States. In 1917 Americans feared that a victorious Imperial Germany commanding the entire resources of Europe and facing no serious challenge from other Eurasian powers might pose such a threat. In 1941 they feared that if Nazi Germany and Imperial Japan were successful, they might do so. After 1945 the Soviets posed the most serious threat, and would have posed even more of a threat had they taken control of the key power centres of Western Europe and Japan. So three times during the twentieth century, the United States marshalled immense resources, paid huge costs and accepted terrible risks to prevent the emergence of a Eurasian power strong enough to threaten the US homeland. This remains America's ultimate strategic objective beyond the Western Hemisphere today. America's security still depends most fundamentally on preventing the emergence of a power elsewhere in the world strong enough to pose a direct military threat to the continental United States, including a credible nuclear first-strike capability.

Clearly, as China's power grows, Americans will ask whether in decades to come it could pose such a threat. If so, countering that possibility – even if it seems rather distant – will be America's primary strategic objective in its relations with China. Yet, as we have seen, for all its immense potential as the world's biggest economy, China's capacity will remain severely constrained. It will be only one of a number of very strong states in Asia, all probably determined to prevent China dominating them. China therefore has little chance of establishing an unchallenged hegemony over its own region. Without that, it would never be able to marshal the resources needed to threaten the United

States. For this reason, advocates of 'offshore balancing,' such as Christopher Layne, have long argued that America could step back from Asia and leave it to China's neighbours to counterbalance its power, prevent it dominating the Eurasian continent, and ensure that it never grows strong and secure enough to threaten the United States.[21] If for some reason they start to falter in the task, America could step back in to bolster and support them. It is a credible argument, but this hands-off approach makes some people nervous. They think it is unwise to leave the task of balancing China's power to others, and see a risk that if China's neighbours failed to constrain it, America might leave direct intervention until it was too late, when it would be much more costly, or perhaps impossible, to contain China's threat.

This, too, is a credible argument, but it is not necessarily an argument for the United States to maintain primacy in Asia. There are many ways for America to stay engaged in Asia, balancing China's power and constraining its military options. Between the extremes of withdrawal under the banner of offshore balancing on the one hand, and the maintenance of perpetual primacy on the other, there are intermediate possibilities, which would offer America the advantages and avoid the disadvantages of each. Indeed, this is what America has traditionally done in Asia. Primacy only became America's aim when it fell into Washington's lap with the opening to China. Before then, America's aim had always been to prevent Asia being dominated by others, not to establish dominion itself. Perhaps it is time to reinstate that objective.

IDENTITY

Many people believe that America's objectives in Asia, and around the world, go beyond supporting its interests in prosperity and security. America should promote values that are both American and universal: it is 'the last, best hope of earth.' American exceptionalism – the sense that Americans have that their country is not just one country among others, but set apart from all others – goes very deep and infuses every aspect of the political personality of American power as we know it today.

American exceptionalism is easy for non-Americans to mock, but in many ways it is simply a sober reflection of the truth. America is unique, and not just – until recently – in its wealth and power. For more than a century, it has contributed to peace and order, to economic development, to political evolution, and to science, technology and art around the world – and all these contributions have been nothing short of exceptional. But the questions nonetheless persist: what does all this mean for America in Asia over coming decades? Is the preservation of a unique role in world affairs itself a prime US purpose in Asia?

On one view, America should strive to remain the leading power in Asia, not because it serves America's economic or security interests, but because leadership is the only role that comports with America's unique nature. That doesn't seem quite enough, though. A sense that one's country is destined to lead others is hardly unique to America, after all. Every great power at some stage believes it is called to lead. To have true moral force, American exceptionalism must amount to more than a desire to hold onto leadership for its own sake, merely because it is flattering to America's view of itself. Most Americans would say that there is indeed something more, and it is about values. They would say that America must lead in Asia because only by such leadership can it promote American values, and the promotion of these values is essential to America.

Sometimes this necessity is expressed in terms of concrete interests: by arguing, for example, that America can only be truly secure in a world that shares its values. But would America be less secure in a world where some countries do not subscribe to all its values, than in a world where it was in bitter conflict with a wealthy and powerful China? The answer is pretty clear. While in theory America might be more secure if its values were more widely shared, in practice the effort to make this happen could easily make America much less secure – especially if it required the imposition of American leadership on powerful states that were inclined to resist.

At other times, America's values are advocated in less practical and more absolute terms: by arguing that America must promote its values not to make it more prosperous and secure, but because these values are good in themselves, and they are so intimately tied to America's identity. If America did not promote its values, it would not be true to them, or itself. Here it is perhaps enough to make a simple point. No one would deny that America should defend and promote its values at home; this is a national objective of the highest order, for which no sacrifice might seem too much. But the promotion of American values in other countries is a different matter. The first may well be judged absolute, while the second is clearly a matter of judgement and proportion to be weighed against other interests and their attendant costs and risks. To imagine that America should sacrifice as much to promote the precepts of the Declaration of Independence in Asia as it would to preserve them at home is simply muddled. To imagine that America's identity is as closely tied up with one as with the other is to imply for America a very expansive identity indeed, with which few Americans, if they paused to reflect on it, would for a moment agree.

The same point can be made about the international order. How absolute is the match between America's values and this order? One common manoeuvre is to say that America's values require the maintenance of the current US-led order in all its details. That is simply a backstairs way of arguing for America to regard the maintenance of the status quo as an end in itself. A more sophisticated argument is to say that US values require the maintenance of the core principles of international order embodied in the UN Charter. As we will see later, I think that is a much more defensible proposition.

The bottom line here is that for US claims about values to have any weight, they need to be backed by a willingness to pay real costs and run real risks to uphold them – because that is what is at stake in deciding America's future in Asia. It is one thing to say that America is willing to enter into long-term rivalry, and thereby run the risk of major war with China, to defend the principle of non-aggression enshrined in the UN Charter. It is quite another to do so to defend every aspect of the current global order. The moral choice that American leaders will face as they decide how to respond to China's rise is not between values on the one side and interests on the other. It is between the value of maintaining a particular kind of order on the one hand, and the value of preserving peace and minimising the risk of war on the other.

When we weigh the merits of America's three options for responding to China in the light of its values, it is easy to see that withdrawal from Asia looks like a poor choice. It should be just as easy to see that determination to perpetuate primacy by competing with China at the cost of instability and conflict is a poor choice too. It is hard to see how that choice would serve America's interests, or indeed its values, better than the third option of negotiating, if we can, a new order in which power is shared and which preserves the most central norms of international conduct while reducing the risk of conflict. Peace is a value, too.

CHAPTER SEVEN
THE REALITY OF RIVALRY

CONTAINMENT AND AFTER

Nothing is more critical to America's choices about China than a clear understanding of the risks involved in each option. The danger that China might become the hegemon of Asia is clear for all to see. The dangers of US strategic rivalry with China are less clear, but arguably almost as grave – and they are much more pressing. Active rivalry between America and China over their future roles in Asia is no longer a future risk, but a present reality. It has not yet reached the point where Beijing and Washington cannot work together and manage bilateral issues between them cooperatively. But it has already reached the point where, for both countries, maintaining and improving their competitive position vis-à-vis the other is quite clearly their principal military and diplomatic priority, and they are increasingly willing to risk damaging the cooperative elements of their relationship in order to gain an advantage.

For China the focus on America as its main foreign policy priority is not new, but dates back to the 1970s, while eroding America's military position in the Western Pacific has been its main defence priority since at least 1996. What is new is China's willingness to acknowledge and assert its ambitions to expand its leadership role in Asia at America's expense, to allow those ambitions to become unambiguously clear to America, and to live with the consequences of Washington's response. Until very recently, Beijing followed Deng Xiao Ping's advice to minimise resistance to China's rise by downplaying both its power and its ambition as much as possible while they grew. But around 2009 – perhaps coinciding with the Global Financial Crisis – Beijing became much more assertive on a range of issues, from international economic and financial affairs and climate change to maritime claims in the South and East China seas. It has become increasingly willing to risk confrontation with Washington over issues, often trivial in themselves, in which America's status as a global and regional leader is at stake. It is seemingly seeking opportunities to undermine that status by putting America in the position of backing down in the face of Chinese power.

For America the switch of focus to China is much newer and more striking. After a decade in which US attention has been firmly fixed on Al Qaeda, Afghanistan and the Middle East, the last few years have seen China move unquestionably to the centre of policy attention. This has been clear not only in the statements and actions of the Obama administration, but also in the responses to them from others, including on the Republican side of politics. Since about 2009, a clear consensus has emerged in Washington that China poses the biggest threat to America's international position, and that responding to this threat is now the highest foreign and strategic policy priority. In the military sphere this has been made unmistakably clear in new strategic documents and above all in the priority given to the 'pivot' to Asia.[22] For a long time the principal task of the Chinese military has been preparing for war with the United States. Now the principal task of the US military is preparing for war with China, and it is being actively reshaped for that purpose.

The most striking sign of the increasing sense of rivalry from America's side has been the shift in the tone of statements by leaders, including President Obama, and the policies Obama has adopted, from the military 'pivot' to the proposal for the Trans-Pacific Partnership as a new framework for economic interaction across the Pacific, intended to exclude China until it is willing to accept America's conditions to join. The word 'containment' has powerful and emotive connotations in American foreign policy. Those who have been shaping American policy towards China in recent years are quick to deny that they are trying to 'contain' China in the way the Soviet Union was contained. At one relatively superficial level, they are right. There are many differences between the Soviet Union and China. There are also many differences between US–Soviet relations during the Cold War and US–China relations today, including, most obviously, the absence of a strong ideological element to their rivalry, as well as the strong economic ties between them. Nonetheless, at a deeper level the parallels are clear and becoming clearer.

As it faces China's growing power, America's policy is to prevent any substantial redistribution of influence and authority in the Asian international system in China's favour while resisting China's challenge to its primacy. It aims to do that by building a military and diplomatic coalition among states close to China in order to prevent them ceding a larger leadership role to China and keep them acknowledging US leadership. That sounds like containment to me. The question we must ask is: where will it lead?

SLOW ESCALATION

One possibility is that rivalry between America and China could keep escalating gradually. If this continues, the two countries will come increasingly to see one another as strategic adversaries. This would be reflected in several ways. They will place growing emphasis on developing their armed forces and in justifying this with regard to the threat posed by the other. Their rivalry will increasingly frame their approach to third-party issues, as each side makes denying an advantage to the other a key aim in managing issues that were otherwise separate. They will increasingly judge other countries in terms of their attitudes to their rival, and such countries will increasingly find themselves forced to choose sides. In short, the relationship will come to take on more and more of the zero-sum qualities of the US–Soviet relationship.

The difference would be that, at least at first, America and China would remain closely interdependent economically. We have never before seen the escalation of strategic competition between two countries that are as deeply economically interdependent as America and China. The optimistic view is that the need to preserve their vital economic relationship will forestall escalation, but, as we have seen, that might not work, especially if the political and policy momentum of rivalry builds up before leaders or public wake up to the economic consequences.

If economic interdependence does not stop the escalation, then a point will be reached at which the countries' rivalry begins to affect their economic relationship in significant ways. That would happen, for example, if one side or both decided that they were prepared to miss out on an economic opportunity for the sake of gaining a perceived win, or of avoiding a perceived loss, in their zero-sum strategic rivalry. Or rivalry might raise sovereign risk to the point where investment and trade decisions started to shift. At such a point, companies from each country will have to factor in the risk of conflict or political disruption in deciding whether to invest in the other country, or lend one another money. It might not be very long, therefore, before escalating rivalry could begin to erode economic inter-dependence, rather than interdependence curbing escalation.

No one on either side of the Pacific wants any of these things to happen. Both the United States and China want to maintain the strong and beneficial economic relationship, and the broadly positive political relationship, which has developed over the past four decades. The problem arises when neither side wants these things *enough* to be willing to compromise on their funda-mentally incompatible expectations, or perhaps when neither side sees clearly how seriously their clashing ambitions threaten mutual interests. The risk of escalation does not arise because anyone on either side is foolish enough to want it to happen, but because too few people on both sides see the risk clearly, or how to avoid it.

How far could escalation go? Unfortunately, there is no rea-son to be confident that it would stop, let alone reverse, before it began to take on some of the characteristics of the Cold War, and thus started to damage both countries – and the wider international community – very seriously. There is little chance that other players in the international system could do much to slow it down, because the two rivals are the world's strongest and richest states: their size and power make it hard for any other country or group of countries to restrain them very much. Moreover, the rivalry is likely to develop a momentum of its own, as such rivalries so often do. Each escalatory action from China hardens US determination not to compromise on the basic differences between them and confirms the need for answering actions of its own. And the further the rivalry escalates, the harder it is to get back to discussion without both sides looking as though they have lost and are backing down. Quite quickly it becomes almost impossible for either side to step off the escalator and start compromising.

FAST ESCALATION

Slowly escalating rivalry is not the only possible trajectory, of course. The other possibility is that rivalry could, with little warning, flame into crisis and even war. Understanding the risk of war with China is central to understanding the choice that America faces. Such a war would be easy to start and very hard to end, and its consequences could be catastrophic for America. Minimising such a risk should therefore be absolutely central to America's objectives as it makes its choices about China. And yet the risk of war between the United States and China has so far featured relatively little in the American debate.

Partly this is because Americans have until recently tended to underrate China's military capacities against the United States. And partly it is because major war between great powers is hard to imagine. We have not seen war on the scale of a major US–China conflict since the Second World War. But that does not mean it couldn't happen: in some ways, it makes the risk greater. So it is important to explore the possibility as best we can.

We should start by recognising that America and China could find themselves drawn into a conflict in the Western Pacific at quite short notice at any time. Several different issues could trigger a crisis that would then spark hostilities with little or no real warning. Taiwan has for a long time seemed to pose the greatest risk, and it remains quite possible that developments in the cross-strait relationship could induce a crisis with very serious consequences. But relations between Beijing and Taipei have been reasonably cordial recently, and while that continues there are other issues that probably pose a greater risk of sparking conflict. They include disputes about sovereignty over islands and waters in the South China Sea; America's conduct of naval hydrographic operations in China's Exclusive Economic Zone; US naval exercises near the Yellow Sea; and disputes between China and Japan over maritime jurisdiction in the East China Sea. In each case, the main motor for disagreement is not the substantive issue, but the way each side sees it as a test of relative status in the Western Pacific. When status is at stake, it is very difficult to accept an outcome to any contest, however minor, that can be portrayed as a defeat for one side or a win for the other. The more intense the rivalry becomes between America and China, the more it will amplify and complicate every strategic interaction, the more each contact will become a test of strength, and the harder it will be to prevent crises escalating. Already questions of status have become so entwined with each of these issues that a relatively minor crisis in any of them could escalate to conflict.

Second, even a relatively minor conflict between America and China would have immense consequences. It would probably change the nature of the relationship fundamentally and permanently. Even if the two sides avoided a major conflict, there would be very little chance of returning to the current pattern of rivalry mixed with cooperation and interdependence. Much more likely, the relationship would short-circuit through to a deep Cold War–style rivalry, as trust collapsed on both sides and the depth of differences became starkly plain. Even a small war, in other words, would permanently dash the hope that the

United States and China could build a stable and cooperative relationship. Everyone's prospects would then darken.

It is also important to recognise that even a relatively minor US–China conflict would have immensely damaging immediate consequences for the regional and global economy. Trade and financial transactions between the United States and China would stop dead, of course, and trade between China and everywhere else would no doubt stop too. Shipping in the Western Pacific would probably cease for a substantial period, and America's allies in Asia and beyond would come under great pressure to stop trading with America's enemy. The consequences for the global economy are incalculable, even if the conflict ceased within a few weeks. If it dragged on for months, the entire structure of global trade and finance would be massively disrupted.

A CRISIS SCENARIO

These risks are best seen by exploring a simple scenario. Over the last few years, America has responded to China's strident assertion of its claims to the disputed waters and islands of the South China Sea by clearly stepping up its support for other claimants, especially Vietnam and the Philippines.[23] As the United States and China up the ante in this way, it has become clear that for both of them the substantive issues at stake are less important than what the dispute symbolises about their respective positions as maritime powers in the Western Pacific. That makes the situation much more dangerous. Both Beijing and Washington are now committed to positions from which they cannot withdraw without conceding a win to the other. If China backs off, America's status as the dominant maritime power in Asia will have been confirmed. If Washington fails to back Hanoi or Manila against Chinese pressure, Beijing's ascendency will have been confirmed, and America's claims to maritime primacy in Asia badly dented. So for both the United States and China there is a lot more at stake now than rocks and reefs, or even oil and gas.

Against this background, what happens if a future China–Vietnam incident in disputed waters escalates? Say a Chinese patrol vessel once again interferes with Vietnamese seismic surveys in disputed waters around the Spratly Islands in the South China Sea, and in response the Vietnamese fire on a Chinese ship. China fires back and a skirmish ensues. China increases its forces in the conflict zone, while Vietnam turns to America for support. America has no treaty obligations to Vietnam, but it has sent Hanoi strong signals of support in standing up to China over the Spratlys. America would therefore face an awkward choice. If it supports Vietnam, it risks being drawn into a conflict with China. If it stands back, it risks damaging its standing in Asia as a reliable bulwark against China's power. The fear in Washington would be that not just in Hanoi, but also in Manila, Singapore and Jakarta, and even in Delhi, Seoul and Tokyo, America's standing as an Asian power would be weakened. Americans would fear that they would be seen to have backed down to Beijing, thereby surrendering a big share of the maritime power that Washington has for so long claimed and exercised in the Western Pacific. The domestic politics of this in the United States would be strident. Saying no to Vietnam might well seem impossible. So they say yes.

Having said yes, what can America do? Fifteen years ago the answer would have been simple. CINCPAC would have sent a couple of Aircraft Carrier Battle Groups steaming through the South China Sea, confident that this formidable display of seapower would deter the Chinese from any further action.

Today it is not so simple. America can still sail its carriers through the South China Sea, but as we saw in Chapter Four, China has a much better chance of sinking one of them now than it had fifteen years ago. The US Navy might calculate that China would not attack a carrier unless US forces attacked them first, but in that case, what use are the carriers? Their presence and vulnerability inhibits rather than empowers the United States, because the need to protect them would discourage action that might escalate the crisis. China could continue to act against the Vietnamese forces, secure in the knowledge that America would not intervene for fear of Chinese retaliation against a carrier. The carrier deployment then becomes more a demonstration of weakness than a show of strength, and all the negative consequences that America hoped to avoid by agreeing to support Vietnam happen anyway.

The brutal conclusion is that once its willingness to support its Asian friends and allies is put to the test, America can only protect its position in Asia by being willing to engage in combat with Chinese forces. So the carriers launch their aircraft and sink some Chinese ships. How does Beijing respond? It now faces the same problem Washington faced a few days earlier: if it backs down, its claims to a leading role as a maritime power in Asia are dashed, and public opinion in China is no doubt outraged. For China's leaders, not responding to the sinking of a PLA Navy ship by the US Navy would seem to be impossible. So they sink an American ship. If they are smart, it would not be a carrier but something smaller. Let's hope they are smart, because once China sinks a carrier, all hope of resolving the crisis would be ended. If they sink a small destroyer, there is still a small chance that, with very adroit diplomacy and great political courage on both sides, it might be possible to pull back from the brink. The chances are, however, that these will either not be in evidence or not be sufficient to prevent governments being swept along both by their own anger and anxiety, and by immense public pressure, towards escalation.

From here the step to major war is short and sharp. As we saw in Chapter Four, under America's evolving operational concept for war against China – the Air–Sea Battle – the United States would start hostilities with a massive strike campaign to destroy China's air and naval forces so that its maritime forces could operate with impunity. While that makes operational sense, it has very grave strategic implications, because it guarantees that any conflict with China immediately escalates to very high levels of intensity, with wide-ranging US attacks directly on Chinese territory. Therefore, this operational concept alone guarantees that the conflict very quickly becomes the biggest war for many decades, and quite possibly the biggest since the Second World War. But America would still be no closer to achieving its overall strategic objectives, however they might be defined. What would count as winning the war that could justify the immense cost of the conflict now unleashed? Even more than most wars, this one would turn out to be easy to start, but very hard to end.

Finally, there is the nuclear dimension. We can only guess about where the nuclear threshold would lie in a crisis like the one we are envisaging. And in fact the threshold is probably as unclear to those responsible for managing the crisis as it is to the rest of us. In the Cold War, the conditions under which each side would resort to nuclear weapons were extensively discussed and – within limits at least – well understood. Between the United States and China these issues are much less clear, and the scope for misunderstanding is huge. Suffice to say that once operations against China on the scale of the Air–Sea Battle were launched, it would be very unwise to assume that China would not consider the use of nuclear forces against the bases from which those operations were being mounted, for instance Guam. As we saw in Chapter Four, China's leaders might well believe that America would not retaliate with nuclear force for fear that China might then launch its intercontinental ballistic missiles against cities in the United States. Who knows if they'd be right?

This sort of discussion can only be speculative, of course, but the speculation is not idle. A wise man once said that those who cannot imagine catastrophe have no capacity to prevent it. America's leaders cannot make a responsible choice about the future of US relations with China unless they clearly understand the risk of war, and how their choices will affect that risk. We have no better way to explore those risks than by trying to imagine what might happen. The risks are not remote or implausible. A choice by America to respond to China's rising power by competing with it for primacy in Asia will be a choice to accept those risks. Anyone who advocates that choice for America is committing themselves to the judgement that those risks are less than the risks of the other options available for dealing with China. That judgement needs to be based on a clear idea of what the risks of war really are, as well as a deep understanding of the alternatives.

CHAPTER EIGHT
A CONCERT OF ASIA

A NEW ORDER

America and China risk becoming bitter rivals in Asia because
they have diametrically opposed ideas about their future relationship and the future of Asia. As we have seen, America wants to
preserve the US-led order which has worked so well for the past
forty years. China wants to move to a new order in which it plays
the leading role. Both, of course, want peace, but they disagree
about how it will be maintained. It is an old story. As Admiral
Jacky Fisher, who built the Royal Navy before the First World
War, said of Europe's rivals at that time: 'All nations want peace,
but they want a peace that suits them.'[24]

How are we to understand and respond to this new world
of risk? In the *Decline and Fall*, Gibbon suggested that Europe's
rulers did nothing effective to save Constantinople from the
Ottomans in 1453 because, among other things, they did not
understand the danger properly: 'by some the danger was considered as imaginary, by others as inevitable,' he wrote.[25] We are at
risk of making the same mistake. Many people believe that escalating competition between America and China is inevitable, and

many others comfortingly assume it is virtually impossible. Strangely, but perhaps not surprisingly, many people manage to hold both views at different times, and even simultaneously. Both views are mistaken, and they both make an intensifying rivalry more likely, because each in its different way discourages action to stop it.

The argument that China's rise makes conflict with America inevitable is most forcefully put by John Mearsheimer.[26] He says that throughout history every rising major power has challenged the established great powers, leading to war, and the same will happen this time. It is a strong argument, but it overlooks the scope for people and governments to shape what happens. The evidence of history shows that it is both very unusual and very difficult to avoid rivalry and conflict when power shifts between great powers, but it can hardly be *impossible* for America's and China's interests to be reconciled without war. That would underestimate people's ability to recognise their own best interests, and to compromise and cooperate with others to promote them.

The central idea of this book is that such an understanding is possible today between the United States and China. Of the three options available, the best way for America to respond to China's growing power is to agree with China to share the leadership of Asia. This kind of order is hard to imagine, harder still to achieve, and if achieved, it would be difficult to maintain. It would hardly be worth considering if the alternatives were not so bad. But if there is any way to avoid both the dangers of Chinese domination and the risks of rivalry, it will be through a new order in which China's authority and influence grows enough to satisfy the Chinese, and America's role remains large enough to ensure that China's power is not misused.

Our task then is to establish what an order based on this kind of accommodation might look like, how it might work, and how it could be built. That is the focus of this chapter. I do not predict that the deal will be done. It is a long shot. More likely, America and China will head further along the path they are already following. They will be drawn deeper into strategic competition, their economic relationship will wither, and the risks of conflict will grow. The alternative described here is not more probable than that, but it is far more preferable.

In an order based on shared power, the United States remains a central player in Asian affairs. Its power balances and constrains China's, protects American interests and enforces vital norms of international conduct. So this is not a matter of abandoning Asia to China, but rather of avoiding that outcome, while at the same time avoiding the risks of rivalry. But this does not come for nothing. America will have to exercise its authority and influence within limits acceptable to China, just as it requires China to exercise its power within limits acceptable to the United States. The hardest part of building an order like this is to negotiate those mutually acceptable limits. It requires a very different diplomacy from anything we have seen for many decades.

This diplomacy would have little in common with the regional forums of recent decades such as the East Asia Summit, Asia-Pacific Economic Cooperation and the various versions of the Association of Southeast Asian Nations. These all reflect the old order in Asia, rather than contributing to building a new one; that is inherent in their nature as large, inclusive bodies in which every country has an equal say. New orders are not built this way. They are shaped in negotiations among the most powerful states – the great powers. Those negotiations do not happen in front of others, as they involve painful and reluctant compromises on key interests and questions of status. Often these compromises occur implicitly rather than explicitly – although the outcomes must become explicit eventually. If Asia's strongest states are to build a new order based on a concert of power, we will have to start with a blank sheet.

DOING A DEAL

Sharing power in Asia is not something America can choose to do on its own. Washington and Beijing must both *agree* to do it. As with any agreement, the essence of any power-sharing deal in Asia is a certain symmetry in the two sides' situations and interests. That symmetry can be hard for many people to see. They view China and America as differing profoundly in the legitimacy of their power and ambitions. Americans believe their country's aim is to uphold the existing order on behalf of the people not just of the United States but of Asia as well, and they believe China's revisionist ambitions threaten to disrupt that order and disturb the peace and stability that is so clearly in everyone's interest to maintain. The Chinese, of course, see a parallel but opposite asymmetry. They believe that China is seeking to exercise its newfound power to remedy longstanding injustices in the regional order, and they see American resistance as an attempt to perpetuate these injustices and inhibit China reaching its full potential.

These conflicting claims to legitimacy are the first thing that must be addressed if there is to be any hope of the United States and China managing their relationship peacefully, and this may prove to be the hardest issue of all. The first requirement of any negotiation is to accept and acknowledge that your counterpart's objectives are, in the broadest sense, legitimate. That does not mean that they have to be accepted, or even respected. But if there is to be any chance of America and China peacefully coexisting as Asian powers, each side will have to accept the *legitimacy* of the other's ambitions. America will have to accept that it is legitimate for China, as its power grows, to want greater authority and influence. Equally, China will have to accept that it is legitimate for America to remain an active player in Asia.

Once we accept the legitimacy of the two sides' ambitions, the broader symmetry of their positions becomes easier to see. Both want to maximise their authority and influence. Both see themselves competing for influence against the other in a zero-sum game in which a loss for one is a gain for the other, so each wants to minimise the other's influence as well as maximising their own. But they both face huge risks from rivalry with each other, and the further each pushes their ambitions for influence, the more intense, costly and risky the rivalry becomes.

Both countries are so powerful that neither can hope to win a competition for primacy outright, so both would be best served by playing for a compromise. Both should therefore seek to do a deal at the point at which further gains in influence are not justified by the higher costs of rivalry. Whether a deal can be done at that point depends on two things. First, whether leaders in both countries understand their situation in this way: whether they see the symmetry in their situations and the possibility of a deal inherent in it. Second, whether their appetites for risk or ambitions for power are so widely different that they cannot be brought to meet at a point of agreement.

A deal like this will always feel like a loss to *both* sides. When two evenly matched powers sit down to negotiate, any acceptable and enduring outcome must leave both sides with less than they had hoped. Both will have had to give away things they badly wanted to preserve. Both will worry that they have given away too much. Each side will be criticised at home for having done exactly that. In successful negotiations between evenly matched powers, it is hard to look like a winner and easy to look like a loser. If one side does feel like a winner, the other side will certainly feel like a loser, and the deal will not stick. The only deals that last are those that leave both sides feeling they have given away more than they wanted.

It will take remarkable statesmanship on each side to navigate both the international and domestic politics so as to reach an agreement. There would therefore be no reason to think there is any chance of a deal being done, were the stakes not so high. Indeed, they could hardly be higher, in two ways. First, economically: a power-sharing deal in Asia provides by far the most promising, and possibly the only, basis for maintaining the intense economic interdependence between the United States and China on which the economic futures of both countries depend. Second, strategically: there would be no chance of the United States and China agreeing to share power in Asia if they did not fear each other as adversaries. Leaders in both capitals will only accept the huge political costs of deal-making to share power because they understand that the inevitable alternative is escalating rivalry, and just how costly and risky that would be.

But in addition, the people who will determine the future of US–China relations will need ideas about how to avoid these misfortunes. The best place to find such ideas is in the history books.

THE IDEA OF A CONCERT

In 1815, as Europe emerged from the Napoleonic Wars, the leaders of its five great powers met in Vienna to negotiate a new post-war order in Europe.[27] Their aim was to reduce the risk of major war among them, because the previous twenty-three years had taught them just how bad such wars could be. The order they created lasted, in different forms, for almost a century. Only in 1914 did the great powers again descend into a full-scale continental war. The century from Vienna to Sarajevo was indeed the European Century. Between 1815 and 1914, Europe enjoyed an unprecedented expansion of population, wealth and power. We still live with the consequences of its collapse a century ago.

The order created in 1815 was called the Concert of Europe. Historians differ over how far that label should apply to the shifting patterns of European diplomacy over the following century, but I am using it to describe the underlying order that prevented engulfing wars throughout the nineteenth century. This was far from an era of universal peace in Europe: serious wars occurred quite often, most obviously the wars of German unification, which culminated in the creation of modern Germany in 1871. But none of these wars escalated into the kind of full-scale continental conflict that marked the years before 1815 and after 1914. Why was that? The concert reflected an understanding among Europe's great powers about their relations with one another. The essence of that understanding was simple: they agreed that none would seek to dominate Europe, and that if any of their number tried, the others would unite to defeat it.

This was a deal among the great powers; middle and smaller powers were not at the table. To qualify for a place was a matter of strength: a country had to be strong enough to pose a potential threat to the independence of the other great powers by seeking to dominate the system as a whole. It had to be strong enough to frustrate any other single power's bid for primacy. That made it strong enough to influence the whole European system and to render unworkable any ordering of the system that did not meet its minimum needs. In other words, it had to be a great power. The main criticism of the Concert of Europe was that it ignored or sacrificed the interests of small and middle powers to the interests of the great. This is true: the Concert of Europe was a very imperfect system that created, or at least failed to prevent, great injustice for smaller states. The only thing to be said in its favour was that it prevented major war between Europe's great powers for ninety-nine years. When we look at the century that followed its collapse, that does not seem a small achievement. Nor did it benefit the great powers alone. No student of nineteenth-century history can ignore the fate of Poland at the hands of the great powers after 1815. But we might ask whether Poland and its people fared worse from 1815 to 1914, or from 1914 to 1989.

The concert was not founded on any abstract commitment to principles of peaceful coexistence or the brotherhood of man. It gained its strength from the clear and very practical recognition by successive generations of European statesmen that the costs of seeking hegemony outweighed the benefits. They knew that power was distributed relatively evenly among a number of strong states, and they were quick to unite against any hegemonic ambitions, because all were eager to avoid being dominated. Moreover, they realised that unrestrained strategic competition carried grave risks of a general war that would ruin them all. The real foundation of the Concert of Europe was therefore the realisation among European powers that they all had a lot to lose from competition for primacy, and a lot to gain from preventing it.

The Concert of Europe might seem to be simply a continuation of the old balance of power system which had characterised the European order for 400 years. But, in fact, a concert of power is very different from a balance of power. A concert requires an agreement, implicit or explicit, among the major players not to seek primacy in a strategic system. In a balance of power the parties do not agree not to seek primacy; the system simply makes it hard for any power to achieve primacy through the spontaneous tendency of countries to unite against any strong power that threatens to become dominant. In other words, it just makes it harder for any party to win, but does little to reduce the intensity of competition or the risk of war: indeed, these are essential to its working. A balance of power is what emerges naturally if the great powers in a system fail to agree on a concert, and it is what happens if a concert collapses, as happened in the years before 1914. By contrast, a concert is an agreement to minimise the risk of war that is inherent in the balance of power system.

A concert of power therefore does not happen naturally. It has to be carefully built and maintained, and this is not easy. There are few successful examples, at least in modern history. Twice in the twentieth century the international community tried to build a global concert of power, once in 1919 at Versailles, and again in San Francisco in 1945. The League of Nations and the United Nations were both conceived essentially as concerts of power. After the failure of the League, the architects of the UN tried to strengthen the concert mechanism at the heart of the new organisation by reflecting it directly in the permanent membership of the UN Security Council. This permanent membership was intended to constitute the world's great powers working together in concert.

Both attempts failed, of course, and the global order degenerated into a balance of power system which led to world war in 1939, and to the Cold War after 1947. The lesson to be drawn from this is that elaborate institutions and formal processes are much less important than the strength of the underlying under-standings among the great powers themselves. When those understandings are strong, a concert can work with very little formal machinery, if any. When they are weak, the most elabor-ate machinery and institutions will achieve little. So when we think about what might be needed to establish a concert of power in Asia in the Asian Century, we should focus on the basic understandings that need to be reached among the key powers, and how they can be reached, rather than on mechanisms and institutions.

ESSENTIAL UNDERSTANDINGS

A concert of powers, then, is an agreement among a group of great powers not to try to dominate one another, but to accept one another as great powers and work to resolve differences by negotiation. It is not an agreement to forgo competition com-pletely, but to limit it. The key limitation is simple: members agree not to try to deprive one another of the status of a great power. Competition among them must not threaten their status as an independent and equal member of the concert. Within this limit, they can compete fiercely. The concert powers of nineteenth-century Europe competed for colonies outside Europe, and indeed right up to the edges of Europe itself – hence the salience of the Eastern Question in the diplomacy of the era. The powers of an Asian concert would no doubt compete for influence in Africa and the Middle East, just as their European predecessors did.

The basic agreement underlying a concert cannot, however, stand on its own. It depends on some fundamental understand-ings that must be sustained if the concert is to endure. I count seven of them.

First, each power in a concert must fully accept the legitimacy of the political systems of all the others. This does not mean that the political systems need all be the same or even similar. The Concert of Europe included an absolutist monarchy (Tsarist Russia), a parliamentary monarchy (Britain) and an intermittent republic (France), as well as political systems in complex transition like the Dual Monarchy of the Austro-Hungarian Empire and fast-changing Germany. In the mid-nineteenth century the political systems of Russia and Britain had as little in common as those of the United States and China do today. The need to tolerate this diversity does not mean that powers in a concert cannot criticise one another's political systems or the values that underlie them. But those criticisms must stop short of questioning the essential legitimacy of another power's state and government.

Second, each power must accept that the views and interests of other powers may – within limits – legitimately differ from their own, even where they conflict directly. The essence of the concert is a willingness, indeed a commitment, to resolve such conflicts by negotiation, and to accept that, in the process, each side will have to make concessions.

Third, each power must accept that members have the right to use force to protect their interests, and to build forces sufficient to do that. Forces strong enough to threaten the independence of other great powers are not acceptable, but those strong enough to enforce interests against other powers are. A concert is not a measure to limit armaments, but if one state achieves a clear preponderance of military strength over another then the concert will be undermined.

Fourth, the powers must share a clear understanding of legitimate conduct. They must be able to identify and agree on the kinds of behaviour that the members of the concert cannot accept and must oppose. Uncertainty about this shakes confidence that the concert will indeed protect its members' most important interests. The main purpose of a concert is to avoid domination by one power, so the definition of unacceptable conduct tends to focus on this. The parties to a concert must agree to resist conduct by any of their number that aims at domination.

Agreeing to these limits in practice is hard. One simple and obvious starting point is the UN Charter, which was drafted specifically to define the circumstances under which the international community would act collectively against states that violated the international order. Thus, we might adopt the language of Article 2 of the UN Charter that requires members to refrain from the use of force, at least against one another.

That may seem too narrow a prohibition. It is appealing to try to turn a concert between major powers into a regime to outlaw all uses of force, but this is impractical and would weaken the understanding. Great powers are not threatened by every use of force, and they will not accept major costs and risks unless their own vital interests are engaged. The more narrow the foundations of the concert, and the more directly they bear on the interests of the power themselves, the more robust the concert will be.

Of course, this leaves middle and small powers outside the concert vulnerable to the predations of the great powers. The question is whether one would scrap the concert idea because of this. That would make no sense unless some other arrangement offered greater protection, and none seems to be in the offing. A concert does not resolve every risk, but it does help reduce the most serious one – war among the great powers.

Fifth, the members have to be clearly willing and able to act against any one of their number who seeks to dominate. A durable concert cannot depend on the goodwill of its members. Their agreement not to try to dominate one another must be reinforced by the knowledge that they have no real choice in the matter, because if one tries, it will face all the others in a fight it cannot win.

Sixth, each power must be willing to acknowledge these understandings to its citizens. A concert will not last unless the understandings on which it is based are explained, understood and accepted by peoples as well as leaders. Otherwise, populist and nationalist pressures will make it impossible to stick to these understandings in the day-to-day management of relationships, issues and crises.

Finally, encompassing all the others, the powers in a concert must treat one another as *equals* – countries which will differ in both interests and values, but which share both an acceptance that each may promote its interests as best it can and an overriding interest in keeping the peace among them all.

This formidable list makes clear why concerts are relatively rare in history. But it also shows why they can sometimes work. It shows they do not survive merely on trust, because members of a concert are constrained ultimately by the power of the other members. But to move from the instinctive dynamics of a balance of power to the mutually interlocking understandings of a concert requires negotiation and mutual acceptance. That process can only begin when the parties detect in one another at least a chance of reaching the necessary understandings. Without fairly clear signs of reciprocation, no power is going to start making the necessary concessions – it will place itself at too great a disadvantage if it finds itself in conflict after all.

That is doubtless why concerts have usually been erected in the aftermath of major wars, when everyone is especially conscious of war's terrible cost. It is sometimes said that a Concert of Asia will only emerge after a major war for this reason. That may be true. But the challenge for Asia's leaders and policymakers is to discover whether it might be possible to marshal the political will to build an understanding without paying the terrible price of a major regional war. Such a war could, after all, be the worst in history. It might be possible to build such an understanding not just on fear, but on hope. If we get it right, the Asian Century offers a glittering prospect for half of humankind. It is perhaps no accident that the Concert of Europe provided the strategic underpinnings for the European Century. The statesmen who created it in 1815, and the generations of their successors who sustained it for so long afterwards, must have been encouraged by the knowledge that if Europe remained at peace, the prospects for everyone were very fair indeed. Such is the promise of a Concert of Asia for the Asian Century.

A CONCERT OF ASIA

To explore how we might apply the idea of a concert to Asia today, we must first consider who would be involved. Today there is a clear Asian strategic system, centred on the great concentrations of wealth and power in Northeast Asia. Who are the great powers in this system? The members of a concert do not need to be equal in power. Some may be significantly stronger than others, but the weakest must be strong enough to veto the workings of the system as a whole if it does not suit their interests. The strongest country must not be so strong that it could easily dominate the others – otherwise it would not be sufficiently constrained by the others to be reliably committed to the concert. To endure, a concert must include all powers that fall within this range. America and China, obviously, but who else will qualify in the Asian Century? There are a number of candidates.

First, there is Japan – still the world's third-largest economy. There is no doubt that Japan has today, and will retain for a long time to come, the strategic potential of a great power in Asia. The key question is whether it will choose to exercise that potential by re-emerging as a great power in its own right in the Asian system.

That would obviously involve a radical and traumatic revision of Japan's national self-image, and there are real questions about whether the Japanese people today have the appetite for such radical change, or whether their political system has the capacity to lead them through it. The evidence of the past twenty years suggests that the answer is no to both these questions. In fact, it would probably take a political upheaval – a revolution of sorts – for Japan to emerge again as a great power in its own right.

But that means the alternatives for Japan are bleak. If it remains a client of America, it will be drawn deeper and deeper into the dilemmas outlined in Chapter Five. The stronger China becomes, the more Japan has to fear and the less it can rely on the United States for protection. Its security would come to depend on the existence of an adversarial relationship between its two most important trading partners. This is hardly tenable.

On the other hand, if Japan ceases to be a US strategic client without becoming a great power itself, it would find itself subordinate to China's power – in effect, a Chinese strategic client. Some people who know Japan well believe that it lacks the will to avoid this fate, and they may prove right. But there seems at least a good chance that Japan's deep sense of its unique identity and history, and its deep fear of Chinese dominion, will impel it to take more active control of its own security.

There can probably be no Concert of Asia unless it does. A concert could not evolve between the United States and China while Japan remains as strategically dependent on America as it is today. As long as Japan acts solely in support of America, America is made too strong for China to accept as a concert partner. Likewise, if Japan became a Chinese strategic client – unlikely though this seems – it would unbalance any concert the other way. The telling conclusion is that a stable concert of power in Asia will only emerge if Japan is willing and able to act more independently of America and join the concert as a great power in its own right. This is one reason why building a concert in Asia will be so hard.

India raises different questions. While Japan's power is in long-term decline, albeit slowly and from a high base, India's is growing fast. And unlike Japan, India plainly sees itself as a great power and is keen to act as such. But it remains relatively remote from the key focus of Northeast Asia. It is therefore possible that a concert limited to East Asia could evolve without India, at least for a while. However, as long as India keeps growing, it makes sense to bring it into any concert sooner rather than later. Moreover, India's strength would serve to make the concert more robust, and its presence at the table as an independent great power would lessen anxieties that it was being cultivated by one or other of the concert parties. On balance, I think India is in.

Russia, on the other hand, is out. As we have seen, Russia is unlikely to function as a great power in Asia for a long time to come. Its power does not require it to be part of the concert, and its exclusion would not seem to weaken it. In effect, Russia in Asia has the status of a strong middle power rather than a great power, and middle powers do not get a place at the negotiating table.

The same goes for Asia's other strong middle powers. Korea – even a unified Korea – and Vietnam seem likely to emerge as very substantial middle powers over coming decades, but my guess is that they will not be strong enough to require a seat at the table. Only Indonesia has the potential to become a genuine Asian great power eventually – but not before mid-century. So, for the time being, our Concert of Asia is a party of four.

COULD THEY AGREE?

The key question becomes whether these four great powers could reach and keep the understandings needed to build a Concert of Asia. What would be required of them? Most fundamentally, the four powers would need to be willing to accept one another as equals – with equal rights and responsibilities in Asia. This will not be easy. None of the four likely members of a Concert of Asia has recent experience in a system of great powers. All will have to change their international outlook, and indeed in some ways their national self-image, to make it work.

This is perhaps most obviously true of America. To build a concert in Asia, Americans would have to be willing to treat China as an equal. It would have to accept China, and the others, as military and political peers, and compromise its interests in Asia to accommodate their interests. It would need to accept the legitimacy of China's political system and acknowledge this to American voters. But at the same time it would have to remain active in Asia, willing and able to use force to resist a bid for primacy by any of the other great powers. It's a very big ask.

But it's a big ask of China, too – perhaps even bigger. China has to forgo its dream of leading Asia. It would have to accept that even as the world's richest power, it will not exercise primacy in Asia as America has done. China's rulers and people would have to come to terms with the fact that while it is strong, it is not *that* strong. They would need to accept that trying to impose primacy over Asia's other great powers would cost more than it was worth, and most probably fail. So instead China will have to deal not just with America, but also with Japan and India as equals. For all their caution, this will not be easy for China's leaders to accept. China has seldom before functioned as a great power in a system of great powers. As Henry Kissinger once wrote, like America it has traditionally aspired not simply to dominate the international system of which it has been a part, but to *be* that system.[28] This will be an historic adjustment.

And it's a big ask for Japan. Many Japanese remain deeply uneasy about Japan acting as a great power again. Some fear that their country will again misuse its power as it did before 1945. Others are reluctant to bear the responsibilities and costs of a leading strategic role in Asia. Many no doubt feel both these things. One can see why: the status quo in Asia has suited Japan very well for the past six decades. But for Japan, as for the rest of Asia, perpetuating the status quo is not an option. The choice is between alternative futures, all very different from what we have known. For Japan, becoming a great power again is the least bad option, but it will be very difficult.

India, too, would have difficult adjustments to make. Largely isolated since independence in its own South Asian strategic system, India has even less experience than China of dealing as a great power with other great powers. Like the others, it will have to reconceive its political personality.

WHAT IT WOULD MEAN FOR AMERICA
LEGITIMACY

What would all this look like in practice for America? What would it really mean for the United States to treat China as an equal great power? First, the United States would need unambiguously to accept the legitimacy of the present system of government in China, including the monopoly of power of the CCP. This would be a big step. Many people would say that America already does this, and has done so since 1972. But in fact American attitudes to China reveal doubts about whether the CCP really is legitimate. There remains a deep-seated view that only democratic governments are truly legitimate, and that it is proper for the United States to support those forces trying to overthrow non-democratic regimes and replace them with democratic ones. This thought, for example, flowed though many passages in President Obama's speech in Australia in November 2011:

> Other models have been tried and they have failed – fascism and communism, rule by one man and rule by committee. And they failed for the same simple reason: They ignore the ultimate source of power and legitimacy – the will of the people. Yes, democracy can be messy and rough ... But whatever our differences of party or of ideology, we know in our democracies we are blessed with the greatest form of government ever known to man.
>
> So as two great democracies, we speak up for those freedoms when they are threatened. We partner with emerging democracies, like Indonesia, to help strengthen the institutions upon which good governance depends. We encourage open government, because democracies depend on an informed and active citizenry. We help strengthen civil societies, because they

empower our citizens to hold their governments accountable. And we advance the rights of all people – women, minorities and indigenous cultures – because when societies harness the potential of all their citizens, these societies are more successful, they are more prosperous and they are more just ...

The currents of history may ebb and flow, but over time they move – decidedly, decisively – in a single direction. History is on the side of the free – free societies, free governments, free economies, free people. And the future belongs to those who stand firm for those ideals, in this region and around the world.[29]

China is not mentioned, but it is clear that it is the principal target of the speech. The first paragraph casts doubt on the legitimacy of the Chinese political system, and foreshadows its collapse. The second commits the US government to helping the process along. The third clearly welcomes this outcome. It is a long time since a Chinese leader has spoken like that of America's political system. Elsewhere in the speech, Obama dismissed the CCP's achievements in raising the material well-being of hundreds of millions of people when he said that 'prosperity without freedom is just another form of poverty.'

Many Americans, and many others, argue that America is right to do this. They say it is right to foreshadow and encourage the eclipse of a political system which, as Obama said in his speech, systematically abuses its citizens' human rights. That reflects a difference in values which American policy cannot overlook.

How far would building a concert of power require America to cease speaking in this way? That is a complex question. Clearly America could work with China to create a stable new order in Asia while still speaking out against Chinese internal policies and events of which it disapproves. But building and sustaining that kind of order will be much harder – perhaps impossible – unless US leaders unambiguously accept China's government as legitimate and forswear any ambition to see it overthrown. There is a difference between criticising a government's policies and actions, and contesting that government's essential authority. Governments can criticise one another and still work together as equals. Governments that contest one another's legitimacy and seek one another's overthrow cannot. As hard as it may be to accept, America would need to confine its comments on Chinese politics within the same bounds as it would expect China to observe when commenting on America's.

This raises some profound questions about the nature of legitimacy. Clearly a regime is not legitimate simply because it has sovereign control of territory and people. To be legitimate, such control must be exercised broadly in the interests of the people being governed, and broadly in accordance with international norms. But this principle needs to be applied with judgement and discrimination. It is easy to slide from the idea that legitimacy depends on how power is exercised, to the idea that we should condemn as illegitimate any exercise of power of which we do not approve.

Some governments seem entirely heedless of the interests of their people – regimes like Mugabe's in Zimbabwe, or the Kim family's in North Korea. They are rightly considered illegitimate. But is the government of China one of these? Surely not. There is much about the government of China that is plainly wrong. It is too intolerant of political dissent and too brutal towards dissenters. But one cannot say that China's government is heedless of the interests of its people, and all the evidence suggests that it is supported by a large majority of them. No doubt many Chinese dislike a great deal about their government, but there is little evidence that the vast majority does not accept it as legitimate. There is no reason why the United States should not do so too, especially when the consequences of not doing so are potentially so grave. This does not preclude concerns about human rights in China, which we will consider in more detail in the next chapter. But there is a big and very important difference between criticising a government's record on human rights and casting doubts on its legitimacy.

CONFLICTING INTERESTS

One way of describing a concert is as an arrangement in which all issues are on the table for negotiation, compromise and peaceful settlement except those that impinge on the stability of the international system as a whole. To build a concert with China, America must acknowledge the legitimacy of China's international interests, even where these conflict with its own, so long as they do not cross this line. Acknowledgement here does not mean acquiescence. Rather, it means being willing to engage in hard bargaining, seeking the best possible outcome but accepting that some compromise is inevitable. This is the way in which trade negotiations are conducted: fierce competition is tempered by mutual acknowledgement that it is perfectly reasonable for all sides to seek advantage at others' expense. Take an issue like the treatment of Iran, on which America and China clearly differ. If the two powers are to work together in a concert, the United States will have to give serious consideration to China's interests in Iran, which are different from America's, just as China should give consideration to America's. That is the only way differences are resolved between equals.

How far does this principle extend? Much depends on which interests we consider critical to the stability of the system. For example, should great powers be allowed a sphere of influence in which their interests carry special, or even exclusive, weight over those of other great powers? This is a more difficult issue than one might think. In theory, spheres of influence seem quite contrary to our modern liberal international order. Russia's attempt to claim a sphere of influence in the near-abroad of former Soviet territories has been roundly rejected on these grounds. But in practice, spheres of influence remain an important feature of the international order, most notably in the Western Hemisphere, where the Monroe Doctrine constitutes America's assertion of a sphere of influence covering the entire hemisphere. India claims a sphere of influence in South Asia. Even Australia has long claimed a sphere of influence among its neighbouring small island states in the South Pacific.

So would building a concert mean conceding a sphere of influence to China in Asia? Obviously not over the entire East Asian region: a central purpose of the concert would be to prevent precisely that. Clearly Japan could not be pressured into a Chinese sphere of influence without ceasing to be a great power and jeopardising the stability of Asia. On the other hand, it would only be realistic to acknowledge that, where the vital interests of other great powers were not directly affected, China might be conceded a sphere of influence – in Indochina, for example. It is a complex and delicate question. Many people would argue that this would be a great mistake and open the way for China to dominate the whole region. But we must realistically ask whether the United States and its allies would insist that their own interests in the full political autonomy of, say, Laos, were worth losing the chance of stable relations with

China over, and taking it on as a major rival instead. What of Vietnam? However, it seems clear that the other great powers could not concede to China a sphere of influence that extended to the waters around China. Beijing sometimes appears to lay claim to such a thing – for example, when it says that 'outside powers' have no role in the South China Sea issue. But to concede that would be to concede more than is compatible with the vital interests of other great powers, especially Japan. Determining the scope of respective spheres of influence would be one of the most delicate and complex issues in establishing a concert of power in Asia.

ARMED FORCE

Washington has long claimed and exercised a unique military posture in Asia based on uncontested sea control and power projection in the Western Pacific. It has also regarded any serious challenge to this capacity as not just unwelcome, but illegitimate. Its criticisms have been framed in terms of transparency, with US officials regularly criticising China for not being more open about the aims driving its military developments. In fact, these complaints about transparency have been disingenuous, because China's objectives are perfectly plain to all. Complaints about transparency have been a way to paint China's growing military capabilities as illegitimate.

This would have to change under a Concert of Asia. Treating China as an equal would mean accepting that America could not seek to impose limits on China's military capability that it would not accept on its own. As such, America would need to accept that it could not maintain a privileged position as the primary maritime power in Asia, and accept China's growing capacity to limit US military options in the Western Pacific. Equally, of course, China would have to accept America's ability to limit China's military options. Given the trends outlined in Chapter Four, this may mean no more than accepting the inevitable for both of them.

The same principles would apply to the balance of nuclear forces. The essential condition of equality would require each great power to have the capacity to deter any of the others from nuclear attack, and none to have the capacity to achieve nuclear primacy through a disarming first strike. Again, this seems to correspond to the situation that now exists and is likely to persist between the United States and China over coming decades, but to sustain a concert the United States would have to acknowledge it. In fact, from the military perspective, a Concert of Asia requires the United States to do no more than acknowledge the emerging strategic reality which it has no capacity to alter, even should it wish to.

NEED WE CHOOSE?

Obviously, the concessions needed to build a stable relationship between America and China are going to be very painful and difficult for political leaders to make in both Washington and Beijing. That leads some people to ask whether such conscious and deliberate concessions are necessary. Perhaps a Concert of Asia could emerge spontaneously, without the need for awkward and unpopular choices. For example, Henry Kissinger, in his recent book *On China*, seemed to suggest that as China grows stronger, the US–China relationship will slowly and even imperceptibly evolve to reflect the shift in relative power, allowing a new order to emerge that accommodates China's ambitions without anyone having to make conscious choices about how the new order should work, and without either Americans or Chinese having to make conscious adjustments or concessions to each other about their status.[30] A kind of strategic 'invisible hand' will guide the choices of governments and peoples to promote mutual self-interest. There is even a historical precedent: the gradual, painless and uncontested transfer of global leadership from Britain to the United States in the late nineteenth and early twentieth centuries.

But the more closely one looks at the power shift from Britain to America, the less reassuring it is as a model. Britain's position then was very different from America's today. In the late nineteenth century, Britain faced growing strategic challenges not just from America, but much closer to home, from the growing power of France and especially Germany; and to its far-flung empire, from Russia and Japan. Britain had no chance to retain its primacy against all of these rising powers, and it was clear from early on that accommodation with America would be easier and less risky than with any of the others, because Britain's interests intersected with America's much less than with any of the others. Later, as America's power grew further and Britain's waned faster, Whitehall was wise enough to accept that graceful acquiescence to American primacy would serve Britain's interests best – as indeed it has.

America today faces fewer challenges than Britain then did. And, of course, it is worth remembering that the transfer of leadership from Britain to America happened smoothly because Britain was, on balance, willing to make way. Gradual change of the kind Kissinger envisaged would require all the major parties to tolerate a lot of ambiguity about their place in the system, because while the process of change unfolds, everyone has to be willing to pretend that nothing much is happening. Americans would have to be willing to allow the Chinese to believe that their ambitions are being realised, and Chinese would have to be willing to allow Americans to believe that they remain in charge. Both would need carefully to avoid situations in which their conflicting views of relative status collided. This will be very hard to do. The issues on which each government will most want to preserve ambiguity will be those on which the other will want maximum clarity. And whatever governments in either Washington or Beijing might wish, their peoples will keep pressing them to assert unambiguously their places in the Asian order.

So rather than leading gradually and painlessly to a stable relationship, allowing things to drift along between Washington and Beijing will much more likely lead swiftly and painfully to escalating competition, as we can already see. If Asia's great powers are going to avoid that, they will need to make hard choices, and explain and defend them to their peoples, against a lot of opposition.

CHAPTER NINE
DEALING WITH CHINA

WHY NOW?

If sharing power is so obviously the best thing to do, America's China choice might seem rather simple. In fact, it is anything but. Sharing power with China runs counter to America's vision of itself and its role in the world, and accommodating an ambitious authoritarian rising power runs contrary to many lessons of history, maxims of policy, principles of morality and common prudence. All these concerns appear to weigh against doing a deal with China. They deserve serious consideration. The first question is: why now? Some people who see the underlying logic of the argument for accommodating China nonetheless argue that it would not be wise to start negotiating a new relationship yet: better, they say, to wait. Some argue that it is not yet clear that China will continue to rise, or that it really will challenge America. While there remains any doubt about this, America would be wrong to offer accommodation to China until its challenge becomes unmistakable. Others argue that America will be in a better negotiating position in a few years' time than it is today. And some worry that if the United States makes concessions to China today on the assumption that it will keep growing, it will be hard to take them back later if China falters. How compelling are these arguments for delay?

In Chapter Three, we explored China's power and ambition. We cannot be sure that China will keep growing stronger, nor that its ambition for influence will continue to grow in tandem with its power. But sheer prudence requires that America's approach to China should encompass the clear probability that its power and ambition will keeping growing for the next few decades as they have for the past few. It would be merely feckless to frame American choices about China on the Micawberesque hope that something will turn up, or that China will turn down. If – as is much more likely – China keeps growing relative to the United States, then time is definitely not on America's side. Ten years from now, on current trends, China's economy will have over-taken America's, its growing economic weight will have increased its regional influence, and its armed forces will be better able to deny the Western Pacific to the United States. It is therefore in America's interests to negotiate a new relationship with China as soon as possible, before the power balance shifts further China's way. In fact, the idea that America should defer negotiation with China until its challenge becomes unmistakable seems anachro-nistic: it overlooks the stark fact that a Chinese challenge to American primacy is no longer a future possibility, but a contem-porary reality. It is too late to say that the Unites States should wait till the challenge materialises. It already has.

And if China does stumble? Does Washington need to worry that if America makes concessions to China now, it will be impossible to take them back later? How hard would it be for Washington to reclaim whatever political and strategic space it had conceded? The whole argument of this book rests on the idea that China will exercise more strategic and political weight relative to the United States in Asia as its power grows. If the shift in power from the United States to China is reversed in future, then the shift in political and strategic weight will be reversed too, and the United States will be well placed to claim back what it might have conceded.

There is a second sense in which time is not on America's side. The possibility of starting negotiations at all is dwindling as the United States and China are drawn into increasingly intense and acrimonious rivalry, as we have seen. The further this goes and the more heated it becomes, the harder it will be for both sides to step back and begin to negotiate rather than compete. These considerations suggest that there is little to lose and much to gain by sitting down with China as soon as possible.

But even if it makes sense to do a deal with China sooner rather than later, one might ask why America should make the first move. After all, China is the one that wants a change in the regional order, so surely it is up to China to take the first step. This is a beguiling argument, because like others explored here it shifts responsibility away from today's political leaders in America and on to someone else. But while leaving the first move to China is politically easier for American leaders, it would not serve America's interests, because it leaves future US security in China's hands, dependent on the policy vision and political courage of its leaders. In fact, it leaves Americans relying on the hope that China's leaders will show more statesmanship than their own. Instead, Washington should do all it can to engage Beijing, so that China's willingness to do a deal can be tested. That means America should take the initiative to offer China as much as it reasonably can to bring it to the table – enough at least to make America's willingness to do a deal on reasonable terms absolutely plain. America should never be afraid that showing itself willing to negotiate is a sign of weakness. As John F. Kennedy so famously said, 'Let us never fear to negotiate.' Of course he also said, 'Let us never negotiate out of fear.' The best way to negotiate is from a clear understanding of one's interests, and a realistic assessment of one's strengths and weaknesses.

The process of negotiating with China will be far from simple. As in any negotiation, the way China behaves will depend on the way America behaves, and vice versa. It can be no surprise that China believes the only acceptable outcome in Asia is Chinese primacy, if America makes it clear that the only outcome it will accept is American primacy. Equally, if America says its freedom and safety depend on the universal acceptance of its model of government, then we cannot be surprised if China says the same – giving the rivalry an ideological element that at present it does not have. All this suggests that it will be much easier to get China to agree to an acceptable order in Asia if America makes clear from the outset its willingness to meet China somewhere near halfway. The essential first step in any negotiation is to make clear that you are willing to negotiate.

A NEW COLD WAR?

It makes sense to deal with China in this way only if the costs and risks of rivalry are greater than those of accommodation. I think they are, but many people disagree. They accept that China is already a major strategic rival, but nonetheless believe that rivalry is preferable to accommodation. This view has been elegantly developed by Aaron Friedberg, among others.[31] It proposes that the United States, rather than accommodating China's ambitions, should seek to thwart them, while acknowledging that this will most probably lead to escalating competition.

This view is based essentially on two judgements. First, it is more optimistic that rivalry between the United States and China can be managed without a high risk of conflict or economic disruption. Second, it is more pessimistic about the chances of forging a stable accommodation with China. In earlier chapters I have argued for the contrary positions: for deep pessimism about the future of Asia under strategic rivalry, and qualified optimism about the chances of accommodation. I will not recite these arguments here. But it is worth looking at the deeper sources of disagreement over these central questions. Inevitably, a lot of our thinking about how to handle China draws on the experience of the Cold War – especially for Americans and Western Europeans, for whom the Cold War was such an immediate and pressing reality for so long, and for whom its end proved such a potent vindication of policies of containment.

They argue that, as long as America stands firm, China will understand that a bigger share of influence in Asia is simply not worth the costs of conflict. This is, after all, what happened in the Cold War. Thanks to NATO's immovable determination to contain Soviet power, Moscow faced a stark choice between accepting the status quo and going to war, and was easily persuaded that nothing it could gain would be worth such a cost. Surely Beijing will make the same calculation, the optimists believe. If so, rivalry between the United States and China should settle into the kind of stability that we saw in the Cold War – and that worked out OK, didn't it?

Well, maybe. In retrospect we tend to understate both the risk of general nuclear war throughout the Cold War, including in its last few years, and the role that sheer luck played in avoiding it until the Soviets collapsed.[32] We should not lightly press our luck again by entering into protracted rivalry between nuclear-armed superpowers. Moreover, we should not assume that Beijing will believe that it faces the same choice as Moscow did. The Cold War stayed cold because Moscow accepted that America's determination to preserve the status quo in Europe exceeded its own desire to change it – was strong enough, indeed, for Washington to countenance nuclear war rather than lose West Berlin. A cold war in Asia would only stay cold if Beijing believed the same of Washington, and that seems highly improbable. For reasons we have explored in earlier chapters, Washington has less at stake in Asia today than it had in Europe in the Cold War, and China knows it. And China has more at stake in changing the status quo in Asia than Moscow had in Europe. The Cold War status quo clearly acknowledged the Soviet Union as a great power and a peer of the United States. Asia's status quo today offers China much less, so the Chinese have both more to gain and less to fear than the Soviets did in the Cold War.

Those who prefer rivalry with China to accommodation also tend to believe that the rivalry will sooner or later – probably sooner – lead to a settlement that favours the United States. In other words, rivalry today leads to easier accommodation in future. For example, Friedberg argues that China's political system will probably liberalise eventually, and when it does, America can safely move from containment to accommodation. He believes both that a liberalised China will be more content with the status quo, and that any concessions will be easier to make to a more democratic regime. This also seems too optimistic.

Finally, there is the central fact that as the Cold War progressed, America became relatively stronger and the Soviet Union grew relatively weaker. That is not happening with China. We have no reason to assume that the history of the Cold War will repeat itself. In every way that matters, China is not the Soviet Union. Arguments for containing China which assume that containment will produce the same result as the Cold War founder on this vital fact.

IS COMPROMISE UN-AMERICAN?

The China choice creates a clash of self-images. Americans see themselves as an exceptional country, to which leadership comes not just naturally, but inevitably. Primacy for such a country is not a choice, but a necessity. At the same time, Americans see their country as a reluctant leader, taking up the burden of supreme leadership as the only way to preserve order for the common good. Primacy for such a country is not something to be desired, but only to be reluctantly accepted and gladly laid aside when it is no longer needed. America's choice about China today is a choice between these two images of itself. In making this choice, Americans will no doubt reflect on which image is truer to the vision of their republic's Founding Fathers. There is a strong argument that it is the second image – the reluctant leader, called from his farm like Cincinnatus and eager to return to it – that better matches the ideals of that remarkable group who so admired Republican Rome.

But America's choice today is more complex than the one Cincinnatus made when he gave up the dictatorship of Rome and returned to his farm. There is a third option, sharing power, which means treating other countries as equals – a world of compromise and hard bargains. Is that incompatible with America's exceptional nature? Americans have long believed that their country is too principled to engage in the shifting allegiances and squalid compromises that typify such old-fashioned, old-world power politics. American policy is not based on interests which can be cynically brokered in this way, but on enduring values and principles which are above compromise. A refusal to haggle and accommodate has always been seen as the American way in foreign policy.

Not surprisingly, perhaps, the reality has not always lived up to this high ideal. And more importantly, the history of American foreign policy tells a more complex story. It shows much more willingness than this ideal would suggest to work with other countries, doing deals and building compromises, to serve both America's interests and its values at an affordable cost. In fact, most if not all of the greatest achievements of American foreign policy have been the result not of untrammelled US leadership, but of patient, open and flexible negotiation and compromise with other countries, large and small. And many of America's greatest foreign policy thinkers and actors – Kennan, Kissinger, FDR, Nixon – have adopted this approach. The idea that primacy is the only form of international engagement compatible with America's exceptional status is belied by their acts and ideas. We need only to think of FDR's creation of the UN and his vision for the post-war order, or of Kissinger and Nixon's opening to China.

CAN AMERICA TRUST CHINA?

Those who favour containment doubt China is the kind of country that America could trust. For many people, China's political system raises automatic questions about its dependability and even about the possibility of reaching and maintaining agreements with it. When the stakes are high, it is important to analyse such concerns carefully to see how far they have substance. At one level we can note that China has a strong record of abiding by its international agreements. But looking deeper we can see two different aspects of the issue that deserve closer attention.

First, there is the question of whether China is the kind of country that the United States can do business with when it comes to building and managing the Asian regional order. Here again analogies with the Soviet Union and the Cold War are easy and persuasive, but misleading.

As the Second World War drew to a close, America tried to build a system of collective global leadership among the wartime allies. President Roosevelt's vision for the post-war order was essentially a concert of the Big Four – initially the United States, the Soviet Union, Britain and China. This vision was abandoned in favour of containment after it became apparent to American leaders that the Soviet Union was not the kind of power with which America could cooperate in this way. It was George Kennan who laid out the argument for the policy switch in his Long Telegram from Moscow and his *Foreign Affairs* essay 'The Sources of Soviet Conduct.' Today these works are remembered mainly for their advocacy of containment, but more importantly they laid the foundations for the critical decision that the Soviet Union could not be trusted to work with the United States and other powers to build and maintain the kind of global concert that FDR had envisaged up to his death. The core argument advanced by Kennan was very simple. The Soviet Union could not be trusted to work cooperatively with America because the political legitimacy of the Soviet regime depended on the projection to the Russian people of a sense of perpetual American antagonism, and hence of bitter strategic rivalry with the United States.

A key question for America today is whether the same judgement should be made about China. Does the CCP's legitimacy in China depend on maintaining a sense of rivalry with the United States? Kennan's argument was based on the fact that the Soviet regime had delivered so little to its people and demanded so much. It is hard to argue that the same is true of China today. The CCP's main claim to legitimacy and to the loyalty of the Chinese people is its achievement in delivering both remarkable economic growth and relative political stability. China's rulers face pressure from their people to assert China's growing power internationally, but that is not the only basis of their legitimacy. China's stability and economic growth give the CCP some room to manoeuvre.

It is quite possible that in future China will change, and its rulers will come to see rivalry with the United States and the achievement of regional primacy as so important that it becomes the sole foundation of their legitimacy. But it is clear that they have not believed that in the past, and do not do so today. That gives us grounds to hope that the United States can reach a deal with China that Beijing would be willing to stick to. Unlike Kennan's Moscow, Beijing does not *need* to keep defining the United States as an adversary. That means there is a chance of negotiating a sustainable order.

The second question is whether, having done a deal, China could be trusted not to keep on demanding more. There is always a risk that once concessions start being made to a rising power, it becomes impossible to stop. It keeps demanding more, and the logic of accommodation leads us to give more away until nothing is left. The lesson people draw from this is a harsh one: the only way to make sure we do not give away too much is to give away nothing. This line of reasoning is emotionally satisfying and can be good politics, but it is based on some important fallacies and leads to bad policy.

Of course China will push for all it can get, and it will keep pushing as long as America keeps making concessions. But we need to be careful not to make two common mistakes. The first is to give in to the illusion that if America just stands firm on the status quo, it will not have to make any concessions at all, and everything will stay as it is.

America's choice today is not between keeping things as they are and allowing them to change: it is between two different kinds of changed futures. In one kind of future, America tries to preserve the status quo and pays the cost of escalating rivalry with China. In the other, America makes concessions at the cost of reducing its role in Asia, but with the benefit of avoiding rivalry with a formidable adversary. There is no chance that if America just stands firm, China will go away and everything will keep on as it has been until now.

The other mistake is that there is no mid-point between conceding nothing and conceding everything. The choice of where to stop making concessions is America's to make, and the answer has more to do with psychology than policy. People fear that the psychology of concession develops its own momentum, leading us to make bigger concessions than we should. This is a risk, as everyone who bids at an auction or haggles in a market-place knows. The secret is to define clearly in advance just how far one is willing to go. The challenge for American statesmanship today is to identify the point at which the United States should stop making concessions to China, and to explain clearly to Beijing where that point is, when it has been reached, and what happens if China keeps pushing beyond it. That needs very careful consideration, because it makes no sense to try to draw the line at any point unless America is truly determined to pay whatever the cost is to prevent China pushing beyond it.

Ultimately, that means being willing to go to war. America should not invest its credibility in asserting a role in Asia's future order unless it is willing to fight China to maintain it: that is ultimately what will stop China pushing for more.

APPEASEMENT AND THE LESSON OF MUNICH

In 1938, Neville Chamberlain of Britain believed he could do a deal with Hitler, satisfying Nazi ambitions for power in Europe while avoiding war, by conceding to Hitler what he was threatening to take by force. Chamberlain called his policy 'appeasement,' and he did his deal with Hitler in Munich. Hitler wasn't satisfied, and war came the next year. Many people today will see the idea of accommodating China's ambitions for more power and influence in Asia as making the same mistake. It is a potent charge. A great deal of debate about foreign policy is conducted through historical analogies, and Munich is the most potent historical analogy there is. That makes 'appeasement' the most powerful word in the foreign policy lexicon – a one-word refutation that can kill off any proposal without further analysis. No wonder it is so often used. Indeed, there has hardly been a major foreign policy question since 1939 in which Munich has not been invoked, including Korea, Berlin, Taiwan, Suez, Cuba, Vietnam, Afghanistan and Iraq (twice). In few of these crises, if any, did the lesson of Munich do much to help make good policy. More often it proved disastrously misleading.

Nonetheless, the lesson of Munich remains potent, and its application to America's choices today deserves to be addressed seriously. First, we need to be clear just what Munich's lesson is supposed to be. The popular view – popular with experts as well as with the public – is simply that it is always wrong to accommodate, to any degree at all, any ambitious power seeking more authority and influence, no matter what the cost of such intransigence.

This assumes that every future ambitious power will be as insatiable as Nazi Germany proved to be, and therefore is certain to challenge our most vital interests eventually. It therefore also assumes that war against it is inevitable if its ambitions are not resisted absolutely, and that if it is resisted absolutely it will back down and accept the status quo. The Munich metaphor thus embodies a curious mix of pessimism and optimism. It pessimistically assumes that China's ambitions are as insatiable as Hitler's were, but at the same time it optimistically assumes those ambitions will disappear if we simply stand firm and refuse to accommodate them. Both assumptions are quite likely to be wrong, and if we accept them uncritically we run a terrible risk of fighting a great power with whom we might have been able to live in peace.

So simply falling back on Munich is no substitute for serious analysis. Before applying the Munich metaphor to our present situation, we have to consider how far China today resembles Nazi Germany in 1938. There are two questions here. First, how sure are we that China is as insatiable as Nazi Germany was? For some people, the fact that China wants any changes at all in the Asian order is sufficient to prove that it is determined to overthrow it completely, as Hitler was in Europe. If China is not willing to accept US primacy, so the argument goes, it must be determined to dominate Asia itself, at any cost. There is no basis for this assumption. No doubt there are some people in China who nurse such ambitions, and in future they could become more influential. But nothing in China's conduct in recent decades provides a strong reason to believe that these are its ambitions today, or that they are likely to become so in future.

Indeed, the evidence points the other way. China is ambitious, but it is also cautious and conservative. It seems willing to balance its desire for increased influence with its need to maintain order, and to avoid too direct a conflict with the United States. Some would cite Chinese policy towards Taiwan as a counter-example. But it is a very big stretch to conclude that Beijing is committed to the subjugation of Asia on the basis of its policy towards what all acknowledge to be part of its territory.

Second, how sure are we that if America stands up to China, the challenge it poses to the regional order will disappear? Part of the Munich folklore is that had Chamberlain stood up to him in 1938, Hitler's authority in Germany would have been destroyed, he would have been deposed by the Generals, and Germany's challenge to the European order would have evaporated. Whether this was true is highly contestable. But in any case it is certainly not much use in helping to shape policy towards China today. It is a matter of power. China today is much more powerful relative to its potential adversaries than Germany was in 1938. It is naive to think that if we just say no to China today, it will back off and become reconciled to the status quo indefinitely.

All this suggests we should be careful about applying the lessons of Munich to America's choices in Asia today. The simple fact is that China is nothing like Nazi Germany. It is both a lot more powerful and a lot less reckless. We will get China wrong if we lazily assume that what might have worked in Europe seventy-five years ago will now work in Asia.

What then *can* Munich teach us? In fact, there are crucial lessons to be drawn, albeit different from the usual ones. To see them we need to dispense with the benefit of hindsight and think about the choices Chamberlain faced, on the basis not of what we know now, but of what he knew then. Viewed this way, Chamberlain's mistake was not that he surrendered the Sudetenland to appease Hitler. Harsh though it is, one can understand his view that the fate of the Sudetenland was not worth a major European war, and Chamberlain clearly believed that this was the choice he faced. But it was equally clear, both from what he said after Hitler absorbed the rest of Czechoslovakia in March 1939, and what he did after Hitler invaded Poland in September, that Chamberlain believed Poland's independence was worth fighting Germany for. His mistake was that he failed to make absolutely plain to Hitler that Britain would fight for Poland. We cannot be sure, of course, but some of the evidence suggests that Hitler was surprised when Britain and France went to war over Poland, and might have held back had he known they would. This suggests that the real lesson of Munich is not that one should never make concessions to ambitious powers, but that one should make absolutely clear where the concessions will stop, and be willing to act decisively beyond that point. The implication of Munich for America today is therefore plain. It is not that Washington should refuse any accommodation with China, but rather that it should make crystal clear where accommodation stops, and be willing and able to enforce that limit.

VALUES AND HUMAN RIGHTS

Finally, we come to a question of values. This remains for many people the ultimate sticking point. To them, the violation of human rights in China means that the idea of sharing power with Beijing runs counter to their deeply held convictions about the way values should underpin foreign policy. China's government is responsible for crushing the Tiananmen Square protests, denying religious freedom, suppressing political dissent and oppressing minorities. Many will ask how America can work cooperatively with such a regime and treat it as an equal.

China's government routinely violates the human rights of many of its citizens. Its leaders argue that open dissent which challenges the role of the CCP would lead to political chaos and social disruption, and it is therefore in the interests of the Chinese people to limit dissent as they do. To the West, China's repression of political dissent seems much harsher than is needed to maintain order. It seems directed more at preserving the position of the CCP against the wishes of the Chinese people. Which perspective is true matters a great deal for the judgements we make of China today. There are three possibilities. One is that the Chinese authorities are right that open political dissent would risk chaos. The second is that they genuinely believe what they say, even if their fears are misplaced or exaggerated. The third is that they knowingly and cynically talk of maintaining order simply to preserve their own power. No doubt the third is true to some degree, but how sure can we be that the first two are not also true to some degree as well? It would be surprising if they were not, when we consider China's history and the personal experience of its leaders. They are more anxious about political and social disorder than their counterparts in the West, and differ in how they strike the balance between liberty and order. There is also an argument that China today, for all its repression, still offers its people more political freedom than they have enjoyed for most of China's long history, as well as a large measure of freedom from domestic turmoil.

This need not mean that the West should agree with China's decisions, but it does affect the judgements Americans make about the moral standing of the Chinese state. Many people will be uncomfortable with such tolerance. They believe that human rights embody fundamental and universal values that cannot be compromised. But is this right? Every society strikes its own balance between security and liberty. Different societies strike that balance in different ways, and many societies strike it differently at different times. Most of these shifts do not reflect a fundamental change in values. Many countries in the West shifted the balance between liberty and security when their perception of threat changed after 9/11, and no doubt they will shift again as perceptions change in future: few would seriously argue that America's values changed after 9/11. So perhaps differences in respect for human rights reflect different situations and perceptions as much as different underlying values.

We do not have China's history, nor do we have its current challenges. No one in the West has tried to manage a social and economic transformation on the scale now underway in China. We should not agree with or approve of everything the Chinese government does, but nor should we too lightly assume that the people of China would be better off – that China would remain stable, orderly and growing, as well as free – if it was governed according to Western precepts.

And how far should we balance condemnation of Chinese violations of human rights against its remarkable economic achievements and the benefits thus delivered to its people? Over the past thirty years, the Chinese government has achieved by far the largest, fastest increase in human material welfare in history. China's economic growth has its drawbacks, but it has provided fuller, more secure and richer lives for something like a tenth of humanity – hundreds of millions of people – in a single generation.

When Barack Obama says that 'prosperity without freedom is just another form of poverty,' he is asserting that this remarkable achievement has no moral value. That is surely wrong. Freedom from Want was, after all, one of FDR's Four Freedoms, and the case for development assistance is based fundamentally on the moral worth of material well-being. Obama might denigrate government by committee, but no government has done more directly to 'make poverty history' than the government of China, and it is hard to deny the CCP some of the credit for this achievement. This does not cancel out China's human rights abuses, but it must carry some weight in the moral judgement we make of the Chinese state and in our view of its fitness as a partner.

THE HIGHEST VALUE

At its simplest, the choice that America faces at the start of the Asian Century is between power and order: does America want order and peace in Asia more than it wants the power that comes with primacy? Of course, this is not a choice America can make alone. China, too, faces a choice between power and order: does it seek to dominate Asia and risk the disorder that will inevitably follow, or will it limit its aspirations for power in order to build a stable and peaceful order? Each side is equally responsible for trying to make it work.

There is both a strategic and a moral imperative to do whatever possible to build a peaceful order in Asia. The strategic imperative is to ensure that if confrontation occurs, America and its allies are sure that China's intransigent determination to dominate Asia is the cause. The clearer this is, the stronger will be the coalition that America will be able to build against China. Because, as we have seen, China's Asian neighbours will be much more willing to go to war to prevent Chinese domination than to support American primacy.

The moral case has been put with perfect clarity by one of the great historians of America at war, S.E. Morison:

> No historian, however, may assume the complete righteousness of his nation or the inevitability of a war. He must ask himself whether a wiser statesmanship might not have averted, or at least postponed, a conflict which brought so much misery to the world, burdened his own country with responsibilities it never wished to assume, and opened up a dark prospect for the future of civilization.[33]

The duty that Morison lays on the historian rests even more firmly on those who make, or try to shape, today's decisions. There is a moral obligation to minimise the risk of war if at all possible. That is not to say that war should be avoided at any cost. One plain lesson of the twentieth century is that wars – even terrible wars – must sometimes be fought to prevent outcomes that would be even worse. But the other plain lesson of the twentieth century is that war among the world's strongest states is a truly terrible thing and to run the risk of such a war, let alone to fight one, for other than the most compelling reasons, is a grave error.

It seems strange that after the terrible experiences of the first half of the twentieth century, we should need to remind ourselves of this again. As happened to the Europeans before 1914, long years of peace punctuated by small and distant wars have dulled our awareness of the horrors of major conflict. It is important to remember, as we explore the China choice, what is at stake.

Ultimately, America's choices about China will depend on its political leaders. They will need to explain what China's rise means, the different options which America has in response, what those different options would cost, and which is best for America. These will not be easy issues to explore, and many people understandably believe that the way politics works in America today makes it impossible to place them on the agenda. If so, that would be a tragedy for America. But I do not think we need be so gloomy. As we have seen, there are already signs, from elder statesmen like Henry Kissinger and present leaders like Hillary Clinton, of a willingness to take these issues on, to acknowledge that America faces choices and to recognise what they are. Their arguments now need to be taken further.

CHAPTER TEN
THE PRESIDENT'S SPEECH

My fellow Americans,

Forty years ago, one of my predecessors went to China and changed the world. He turned the world's most populous country from a bitter enemy of America into a cautious friend. In doing so, Richard Nixon brought China into the global economy. And with that, China's people began to transform their material welfare, just as ours was transformed by the Industrial Revolution 200 years before. Nixon, and America, made a vital contribution to transforming China's economy, and now China's economy is changing the world, which in turn has great consequences for America.

Those consequences are what I will speak about today. We need to understand them and debate how America should respond to them in the years ahead. Today we have a fast-growing and increasingly complex relationship with China. The management of that relationship, day to day and issue by issue, has become, quite rightly, one of our highest foreign policy priorities, and in many ways a great foreign policy success. But if we are to get this relationship right, and it is vital for America that we should, we need to look beyond the day-to-day issues and take a broader view of the kind of relationship we should aim to build with China in years to come.

The choices we make about this may prove to be as momentous, and as difficult, as any in our history. They are difficult because they go to the very heart of how we see ourselves as a country. They are momentous because they will help decide whether America will live in peace, or else be drawn into a deep rivalry that could darken our future, perhaps for decades, perhaps for generations.

We need to make those choices soon, before the tide of events starts to sweep our options away – as indeed is already happening. It might be possible for today's political leaders to duck these hard choices, but if we do, we risk leaving our successors with no choices to make, and America much poorer and less secure than it is now, and than it can and should be in future. That cannot be right, and I will not do it.

CHINA'S RISE

There is a truth we need to grasp. Within a few years, it appears, China's economy will be bigger than America's on some measures. Within a couple of decades, it will be bigger than ours on any measure. We will no longer have the world's most powerful economy.

Ultimately, this is a matter of numbers. America's economy has been the world's biggest for 130 years because our workforce is both very big – the third biggest in the world – and very productive. China has many more workers, but they have been much less productive, and so its economy has been smaller than ours. But China's productivity has grown remarkably over the past three decades. They have been having their own Industrial Revolution. With a workforce four times as large, China needs only one-quarter our per capita productivity to overtake us and become the largest economy in the world. That is what is now happening.

This change is not about America. It is about China. America remains, in itself, as strong, resilient and creative as it has always been. But if we assumed that America would always, under any circumstances, remain the world's largest economy when China had the world's largest workforce, it could only have been because we believed that Chinese workers could never, under any circumstances, become even a quarter as productive as we are. And how could we ever have believed this?

Well, many of us have believed it because of China's political system, which is so different from our own. We have held firm to the idea that only a system like ours can unleash the full creativity of a people. I share that belief. And yet we simply cannot ignore the fact that China's government, for all its faults, has presided over the greatest increase in material welfare in history.

Perhaps it will not last. Perhaps China's people will demand more political freedom and participation from their rulers. But if they do – and for many of us it is an article of faith that they will – will that slow their growth in the long run? If the people of China do indeed take the path to democracy, it is more likely – once the turbulence subsides – to strengthen their economy than to weaken it.

Many Americans are in denial about this immensely important change in our international situation. Many of us assume that America's economy will remain the world's biggest forever, simply because we are America. We must not let such self-delusion pass for patriotism. America was not founded on illusion or built by self-deception. It was founded and built by men and women who combined high ideals with a practical grasp of facts. To secure America's future, we must emulate them.

THE NEW ASIA

As China's economy grows, the other dimensions of its power will grow too. We need to recognise this, but we need also to keep it in perspective. China will remain a very strong country, but it will never rule the world. It will have to deal with many other strong states – Japan, India, Russia, the EU and, of course, the United States. Unlike us, it will have little ability to project its military power over the seas, even in the Western Pacific. While its interests will expand around the world, it will remain focused on East Asia.

But as China's power grows, I believe it will want to be a great power again, and to be treated as a great power by others. It would be very surprising if it did not.

That raises a question, for the Chinese and for the rest of the world. How will China use its power? Will it be a harsh bully or a cooperative partner in a regional order? The answers are not yet clear.

One thing, however, is clear. China's ambitions are not compatible with the old order, the one that has kept the region stable, peaceful and prosperous for four decades since Nixon met Mao. The reason is simple. The foundation of Asian order over these decades has not just been American power. That has been essential, but so too has the attitude of Asia's other major countries. Since 1972, America's role as the leader of Asia has been uncontested by any other major power.

We have been not just *a* leader in Asia but *the* leader in Asia. But today we face a new reality. China has begun unmistakably to contest American primacy in Asia and the regional order that has been built on it.

The choice America faces today is how we respond to China's challenge to our leadership of Asia. I believe we have just three alternatives.

First, we can withdraw from Asia in the face of the challenge. There have always been voices in America arguing against accepting the heavy burden of leadership abroad, and we will hear them again. But the counter-arguments remain as strong today as they have ever been. Withdrawing from Asia would leave it to be either dominated by China, or devastated by the rivalry of Asia's great powers. This would threaten both America's security and its economy. There is no peaceful and prosperous future for Asia without a strong US presence, and there is no peaceful and prosperous future for America without a peaceful and prosperous Asia.

Second, we can push back against China's challenge, aiming to maintain our supremacy and compelling China to accept it. For many this is a natural, instinctive response. And if China is determined to dominate Asia by force, it will be the right response. But we should be under no illusions about its cost. China will not simply back down if America pushes back. It would push back at us, and we would push back again in turn. In this fashion, America would find itself in a new and dangerous era of rivalry.

China is not the Soviet Union. It is more formidable because its economy works. Any decision to take the path of strategic rivalry with China must weigh fully the risks and costs. Such a path would carry the real risk of conflict with a nuclear-armed power. That is a very serious risk. America has faced and accepted such risks before. We did so during the Cold War, because we believed the Soviet Union posed a threat to our peace and safety, and that this threat could be met no other way. We will do so again if we face a similar danger. But we would not be justified in doing so unless the threat was plain and there were no alternatives. We are not in that position today with China. We have another option.

The third option is to seek an agreement with China about a new order in Asia, an order that would allow China a bigger role, but preserve a major role for America in keeping Asia secure.

By remaining engaged, America will balance China's power and help to ensure that its power is not misused. By stepping back from primacy and allowing China a bigger role, we will seek an accord that avoids the risks of rivalry, while preserving America's key interests. China's choice
The essence of such an accord is simple. America and China would share power in Asia as equal partners in a joint regional leadership. That does not mean we would agree about everything, but it does mean we would manage our disagreements carefully.

Such a deal would depend as much on China as it does on us. China would have to accept that it will not be able to take over the leadership of Asia, as I'm sure many Chinese hope and expect. It would require them to accept that their country, for all its wealth and strength, will be subject to the checks and balances imposed by American power.

Many in China would not want to accept this state of affairs. They would argue that China should push America out of Asia and take its place as Asia's primary power. To them I have a clear message: America will not accept Chinese primacy. We do not believe that such primacy would be accepted by China's neighbours in Asia. If now, or in the future, China tries to impose it upon them by force or other forms of pressure or intimidation, America will lead them in resisting China. America in the past has shown how steadfast it can be in upholding a free and open international order in Asia, as elsewhere. It will be no less steadfast in future.

But if China is willing, America will work with it as an equal partner in a shared leadership to build and maintain, with other countries, an international order in Asia that conforms to the broad principles laid down in the UN Charter.

Will China agree? If China's leaders are wise, they will see that a shared leadership with America, while less than many of their people might want, is a big step forward. And they will see that to try to gain more – to try to push America out of Asia and take sole leadership – will not work and will put at risk all they have achieved, and all their hopes for China's future.

AMERICA'S CHOICE

America, too, faces a hard choice. Many people will say that dealing with China as an equal is incompatible with our unique nature as a country and a people. Throughout our history we have seen ourselves not as a country like other countries, but as a nation apart. An exceptional country. This has always posed a profound dilemma for our foreign policy: how do we reconcile our sense of exceptionalism with the need to work as a nation among other nations in the international community? And how do we remain true to our exceptional nature while working with the world as it is? The answer has always been that we must deal realistically with the world as we find it, or sacrifice our own interests and those of wider humanity.

Even so, many will say that never before in our history have we dealt with any country as an equal in the way I am proposing we deal with China. That is true. But never before in our history have we encountered a country like China – a country with the potential to become as rich and strong as China is set to do.

America is going to have to deal with the world differently from now on, not because America has changed, but because the world is different.

Many will say that we did not deal with the Soviet Union this way. We were fierce in our refusal to accommodate the Soviets. We committed ourselves to containing their influence, helping ultimately to bring down their regime. That is true, but it is also true that first, before containment, America did all it could to draw the Soviets into just the kind of cooperative international order that I am proposing today.

Towards the end of the Second World War, FDR offered to treat the Soviets and the other great powers as equals and share global leadership with them through the United Nations. Only after Moscow showed it was not willing to accept that offer did we take the terrible and necessary step to enter the Cold War. We should never forget what a difficult and dangerous path that was and how easily it could have ended in unimaginable disaster.

Many will say that America cannot deal with China as an equal because its values are so different from ours. That is a critical difference – in many ways the heart of our argument. Many bad things happen in China. China's government suppresses political dissent, denies religious freedom and perpetuates a political system that deprives people of the right to choose their own government. We should deplore these things, and I do.

In justice, however, we should also acknowledge that many good things are happening in China. Hundreds of millions of Chinese live better, fuller lives than their parents could have dreamed of because of the economic growth that China has achieved. Better homes, better schools, better food, better jobs, better healthcare – these material things have real moral value, and it would be dishonest not to acknowledge this achievement.

Treating China as an equal does not mean that we should ignore the bad things that happen. It means that we should consider carefully what kind of relationship would be best for the people of America, and best for the people of China, and best for people everywhere. The choices we face about our future with China have real consequences for the kind of world we will live in.

Those who say that the weight of values lies on only one side of this argument forget that peace is a value too. What will future generations think if we now turn away from the prospect of preserving peace by building a new understanding with China? Will they see that as a moral choice?

Ultimately, the big decisions about foreign policy end up being about us. How we choose to relate to others depends on how we see ourselves. When we consider whether to compete with China for leadership in Asia, or to seek a way to work with China to build a new order there, we need to ask ourselves why leadership matters. Have we accepted the burdens of leadership because that has been the best way to keep America safe and prosperous, and to help Asia become safe and prosperous too?

Or do we see it as an end itself? Is America today a country that can only conceive of itself as the world's unchallengeable superpower? It was not always so. Once Americans accepted the burden of leadership because it was the only way to keep America safe and the world at peace. But they also recognised that in time a new order could arise in which the United States worked with others as equal partners to keep the world stable and prosperous.

President Richard Nixon had such a vision before he went to China. In 1972 he told *Time* magazine, 'I think it will be a safer world and a better world if we have a strong, healthy United States, Europe, Soviet Union, China, Japan, each balancing the other.'

And President Bill Clinton said a decade ago: 'America has two choices. We can use our great and unprecedented military and economic power to try to stay top dog on the global block in perpetuity. Or we can seek to use that power to create a world in which we are comfortable living when we are no longer top dog on the global block.'

Today we confront that choice. I think most of us would agree that America's political system has not been at its best these past few years. The tougher we politicians have talked, the more reluctant we have been to face tough facts and take tough decisions. Perhaps we feel that America is so strong that we do not need to see the world as it really is. That would be a historic mistake, and contrary to America's true strengths and virtues. We need now as a country to debate our future with China carefully, soberly, responsibly and realistically. America's future depends on it.

May God bless the United States of America.

ENDNOTES

1. There is a wealth of work on China's economic growth and future trajectory. A neat summary of comparisons between the United States and China can be found in 'Economic Focus: How to Get a Date: The Year When the Chinese Economy Will Truly Eclipse America's is in Sight,' *The Economist*, 31 December 2011. An interesting set of long-range projections can be found in Willem Buiter and Ebrahim Rahbari, 'Global Growth Generators: Moving Beyond "Emerging Markets" and "BRIC,"' *Citibank Global Economics View*, 21 February 2011, https://ir.citi.com/wWU9p6kOZ2tAOkgnnXB9YkhuHxQvvYN7dNazx QR26NPgMQRorAmvPw%3D%3D.

2. See, for example, Barack Obama, 'Remarks by the President in the State of the Union Address,' Washington DC, 24 January 2012, http://www.whitehouse. gov/the-press-office/2012/01/24/remarks-president-state-union-address; 'Mitt Romney Delivers Remarks on U.S. Foreign Policy,' speech at The Citadel, 7 October 2011, http://www.mittromney.com/blogs/mitts-view/2011/10/ mitt-romney-delivers-remarks-us-foreign-policy.

3. This is not the place for a detailed bibliography of American writing on US–China relations. Suffice to say that among the contemporary US authors whose works (and in some cases conversations) have shaped my thinking on these issues, I'd mention especially Andrew Bacevich, Ernest Bower, James Fallows, Aaron Friedberg, Bates Gill, Bonnie Glasser, Brad Glosserman, Michael Green, Nina Hachigian, Robert Kaplan, Charles Kapuchan, Paul Kennedy, Henry Kissinger, Christopher Layne, Ken Leiberthal, Walter Russell Mead, Thomas Mahnken, John Mearsheimer, Evan Medeiros, Joseph Nye, Jonathan Pollack, Barry Posen, J. Stapleton Roy, David Shambaugh, Michael Swaine, Daniel Twining, Stephen Walt, Toshi Yoshihara and Fareed Zakaria.

4. Barack Obama, 'Remarks by President Obama to the Australian Parliament,' Canberra, 17 November 2011, http://www.whitehouse.gov/the-press-office/2011/11/17/remarks-president-obama-australian-parliament.

5. Paul Kennedy, 'A Time to Appease,' *The National Interest*, July–August 2010, http://nationalinterest.org/article/a-time-to-appease-3539; Henry Kissinger, 'The Future of U.S.–Chinese Relations: Conflict is a Choice, Not a Necessity,'

Foreign Affairs, March–April 2012, http://www.foreignaffairs.com/
articles/137245/henry-a-kissinger/the-future-of-us-chinese-relations.

6. Henry Kissinger, *On China*, UK and US: Penguin, 2011.

7. Hillary Rodham Clinton, 'Remarks at the U.S. Institute of Peace China
    Conference,' US Institute of Peace, Washington DC, 7 March 2012, http://
    www.state.gov/secretary/rm/2012/03/185402.htm.

8. Richard M. Nixon, 'Asia after Viet Nam,' *Foreign Affairs*, Vol. 46, No. 1,
    October 1967, p. 111.

9. See, for example, World Bank, *China 2030: Building a Modern, Harmonious and
    Creative High-Income Society*, Development Research Center of the State
    Council, the People's Republic of China, http://www.worldbank.org/content/
    dam/Worldbank/document/China-2030-complete.pdf.

10. 'Economic Focus: How to Get a Date,' *The Economist*.

11. Organisation for Economic Co-operation and Development statistics, http://
    stats.oecd.org/Index.aspx?datasetcode=SNA_TABLE1.

12. John Mearsheimer, *The Tragedy of Great Power Politics*, New York: Norton,
    2001; Niall Ferguson, *Empire: The Rise and Demise of the British World Order and
    the Lessons for Global Power*, New York: Basic Books, 2003.

13. Richard B. Strassler (ed.), *The Landmark Thucydides*, New York: Touchstone
    Books, 1998, p. 16.

14. Toshi Yoshihara & James R. Holmes, *Red Star over the Pacific: China's Rise and
    the Challenge to U.S. Maritime Strategy*, Annapolis, MD: Naval Institute Press,
    2010.

15. David A. Shlapak, David T. Orletsky, Toy I. Reid, Murray Scot Tanner & Barry
    Wilson, *A Question of Balance: Political Context and Military Aspects of the China-
    Taiwan Dispute*, Santa Monica, CA: RAND Corporation, National Security
    Research Division, 2009, http://www.rand.org/pubs/monographs/MG888.

16. Stockholm International Peace Research Institute, *SIPRI Yearbook 2011:
    Armaments, Disarmament and International Security*, www.sipri.org/
    yearbook/2011/files/SIPRIYB11summary.pdf.

17. Julian Corbett, *Some Principles of Maritime Strategy*, London: Longmans, Green,
    1911.

18. General Norton A. Schwartz, USAF & Admiral Jonathan W. Greenert, USN,
    'Air–Sea Battle: Promoting Stability in an Era of Uncertainty,' *The American
    Interest*, 20 February 2012, http://www.the-american-interest.com/article.
    cfm?piece=1212; Department of Defense, 'Joint Operational Access Concept,'
    Version 1.0, 17 January 2012, http://www.defense.gov/pubs/pdfs/JOAC_Jan%20
    2012_Signed.pdf.

19. See, for example, Hugh White, 'Stopping a Nuclear Arms Race between
    America and China,' *Lowy Institute Policy Brief*, Lowy Institute for
    International Policy, Sydney, 17 August 2007, p. 18, http://lowyinstitute.
    cachefly.net/files/pubfiles/White%2C_Stopping_a_nuclear_arms_race.pdf;
    Hugh White, 'Nuclear Weapons and American Strategy in the Age of Obama,'
    Lowy Institute Analysis, 21 September 2010, http://lowyinstitute.cachefly.net/
    files/pubfiles/White%2C_Nuclear_weapons_web.pdf.

20. This is the view developed by Aaron Friedberg in *A Contest for Supremacy:*

China, America, and the Struggle for Mastery in Asia, New York: Norton, 2011.

21. Christopher Layne, 'From Preponderance to Offshore Balancing: America's Future Grand Strategy,' *International Security*, Vol. 22, No. 1, Summer 1997, pp. 86–124, http://www.jstor.org/stable/2539331.

22. See, for example, Department of Defense, 'Sustaining U.S. Global Leadership: Priorities for 21ˢᵗ Century Defense,' January 2012, http://www.defense.gov/news/Defense_Strategic_Guidance.pdf.

23. Carlyle A. Thayer, 'The United States and Chinese Assertiveness in the South China Sea,' *Security Challenges*, Vol. 6, No. 2, Winter 2010, pp. 69–84, http://www.securitychallenges.org.au/ArticlePDFs/vol6no2Thayer.pdf. For an interesting analysis of a US–China conflict over Taiwan, see Richard C. Bush & Michael E. O'Hanlon, *A War Like No Other: The Truth About China's Challenge to America*, Hoboken, NJ: Wiley, 2007.

24. Jan Morris, *Fisher's Face*, London: Penguin, 1996.

25. Edward Gibbon, *The Decline and Fall of the Roman Empire*, Everyman's Library, 1910, Vol. 6, p. 482.

26. John Mearsheimer, *The Tragedy of Great Power Politics*.

27. The Concert of Europe has been studied extensively, and its application to Asia has been discussed by a number of recent writers, including Evelyn Goh, 'The US–China Relationship and the Asia-Pacific Security: Negotiating Change,' *Asian Security*, Vol. 1, No. 3, 2005, pp. 216–44; Amitav Acharya, 'A Concert of Asia?', *Survival*, Vol. 41, No. 3, Autumn 1999, pp. 84–101; and Richard K. Betts, 'Wealth, Power and Instability: East Asia and the United States after the Cold War,' *International Security*, Vol. 28, No. 3, Winter 1993–94, pp. 34–77; Douglas T. Stuart, 'Towards Concert in Asia,' *Asian Survey*, Vol. 37, No. 3, March 1997, pp. 229–44.

28. Henry Kissinger, *Diplomacy*, New York: Simon & Schuster, 1994, p. 21.

29. Barack Obama, 'Remarks by President Obama to the Australian Parliament.'

30. Henry Kissinger, *On China*.

31. Aaron Friedberg, *A Contest for Supremacy*.

32. See, for example, Robert Gates, *From the Shadows: The Ultimate Insider's Story of Five Presidents and How They Won the Cold War*, New York: Touchstone Books, 1997, Chapter 14 ('1983: The Most Dangerous Year').

33. S.E. Morison, *History of US Naval Operations in World War Two: The Rising Sun in the Pacific, Volume III: 1931–April 1942*, Boston: Little, Brown and Company, 1950, p. 3.

INDEX

Entries under 'China' and 'United States' have been kept to a minimum. In general, aspects of their activities or relationship have been entered directly rather than as sub-headings under the respective countries, e.g. 'economic interdependence' and 'nuclear weaponry'.

first strike option, 77–8
  implications for allies, 77
Nye, Joseph, 43

Obama, Barack
  on human rights, 168–9
  and rivalry with China, 115
  speech to Australian Parliament
    role in Asia, 8–9
    unique legitimacy of democracy, 143–4
On China (Kissinger), 149–50
One China policy, 95
Open Door policy, 15–16, 17

patriotism, 46–8
Peloponnesian War, 57
Perry, Matthew, 13
Philippines, 16
pivot to Asia, 114–15
political systems
  China, 34–40, 174
    future scenarios, 37–40
    legitimacy, 143–6
      see also human rights, in China
    stresses, 37–9
  legitimacy, 135
  models for economic success, 35
power
  China, 40–5
    constraints, 107–8
    related to economic weight, 41–3
  and Concert of Europe, 131–2
  interests and objectives compared, 66
  its nature, 41
  United States, 40–1
    projection, 17, 44–5, 63
power sharing, 5, 126–8
  benefits, 130
  implications
    for China, 177–8
    for United States, 143–9, 178–81
  reaching agreement, 128–30
productivity, 28–30, 173–4
  China, 32–3
    possibilities, 28–31

regional leadership
  related to international stability, 48–50
  see also leadership in Asia
resources access *see* access to resources
rivalry *see* strategic competition
role in Asia (US), 11–27
  1972 deal, 19–23
  access to markets, 106
  competition, 100–3
    consequences, 101–3
    scenarios, 101–3
  identity, 108–11
  imperatives, 98–9
  objectives, 104–12
    prosperity, 105–6
    security, 106–8
  options, 98–104, 176–7
    competition, 100–3, 176–7
    power sharing, 103–4, 177–81
    withdrawal, 99–100, 111–12, 176
  post Cold War, 23–7
  power sharing, 103–4
  promoting values, 109–10
  reasons for presence, 104–5
  road to primacy, 13–19
  sharing power, 103–4
  uncontested primacy, 11–13
  withdrawal, 99–100, 111–12
Roosevelt, Theodore, 16
Russia
  and Concert of Asia, 140–1
  economic fragility, 87
  effect of US–China deal (1972), 20, 22–3
  European priorities, 88
  role in power politics of Asia, 87–8
  strategic potential, 58
Russo-Japanese War (1904-05), 16

sea control
  China's non-achievement, 70–1
  compared with sea denial, 67
  United States, 63
    Chinese challenge, 65
sea denial, 67, 70–1
sea power, 63
  Chinese maritime capability, 64–8